101 Crafty Cats

Also by Melinda Coss

101 Greeting Cards
Big Softies: 35 Great Designer Knits in Mohair

101
Crafty Cats

(and how to make them)

Melinda Coss

Aurum Press

First published 1994 by Aurum Press Limited,
25 Bedford Avenue, London WC1B 3AT

A catalogue record of this book is available from the British Library.

ISBN 1 85410 340 7

10 9 8 7 6 5 4 3 2 1
1998 1997 1996 1995 1994

Design by Don Macpherson
Photography by Peter Letts and Mike King
Printed in Spain by Grafos SA, Barcelona

Extracts from 'The Old Gumbie Cat' and 'The Song of the Jellicles', *Old Possum's
Book of Practical Cats*, reproduced with the kind permission of Faber and Faber
Limited.

Contents

*With sincerest apologies
to Jazz the poodle*

Acknowledgements

The author wishes to thank the following creatures for their remarkable contributions to this work:

Paddy Murphy, for commissioning it; Geraldine Berkowitz for pawing through it; Priscilla, for sitting on it; Sparky, for walking over it, and Comet, for dragging a mouse across it. Kind thanks also to Sheila Murphy for purring at the right moments, Judy Newman for twitching her nose and coming up with great ideas, Justine Coss for squashing lots of bits of wet paper into fantasmagorical pussy cats, Isobel Copus for knit picking, Janetta Turgel for her cat prints, Kate Bartholo'mew' for designing and making the two gorgeous rag rugs, the wonderful Quilters of Penpompren, Penny Newman for her barge painting, Paula Murray for her exquisite papier mâché sculptures, Jeanette Hall for a stitch in time, and my scratching post Pat Groves. Thanks also to my newly acquired grandaughter 'Dusty Sunshine' – the cat from hell.

Introduction

I just couldn't help myself – during the six months it has taken to create this book every word I have come across seems to include, rhyme with or sound like C-A-T, P-U-R-R or M-E-O-W. The result is an endless collection of the most awful puns interspurrsed with lots of crafty projects that I hope you will enjoy making.

The main purr-puss of *Crafty Cats* is to demystify the techniques of various crafts and to show readers how to translate the bits and bobs they have lying around into useful and decorative cats of all shapes and sizes. The basic skills required are covered briefly, but you do not have to be a creative genius to make any of the projects in this book. If you find you enjoy a craft such as decoupage or papier mâché, there are a number of books available that will develop your skill and lead you on to bigger and better things. Many of the projects are suitable for children and there are some woodcraft ideas that are designed for the do-it-yourselfer, be she male or female. If a finished project appears complicated, the complexity is not in the creation of the object itself but in the skill of the decorator. For example, Paula Murray's cats on pp.19–21 are exquisitely painted, but if you don't feel you could match her standard, copy black and white cat markings from a book or photograph to simplify the process. I have also included a section on how to draw a cat, which you should look at before beginning. I often find that if I understand how something is put together it becomes much easier to reproduce. It is simply the way you look at an object or animal that determines your skill in painting or drawing it.

Finally, how can I end this introduction without talking about cats – in fact, how could I do anything without the knowledge that my furry friends are waiting at home to amuse, comfort or annoy me? Life just wouldn't be the same without them.

A Cat Alphabet

Cheshire Cat as portrayed in *Alice in Wonderland* considered himself to be quite mad because, unlike the dog, he growled when pleased and wagged his tail when angry. There was once a cheese in Cheshire stamped with a grinning cat's face: perhaps this is where Lewis Carroll got his inspiration.

Egypt was undoubtedly responsible for turning wild cats into domestic creatures. In return for the care and concern offered by the Egyptians, the wild cat protected her owner from rodents, snakes and river beasts and achieved considerable status. Along the career ladder, the cat took over the job of watching the temple and was eventually promoted to Goddess of Maternity in the figure of Bastet.

Abyssinian cats are ruddy or red and sing beautifully. They are free-spirited intellectuals resembling in style and temperament the sacred cats of ancient Egypt. Known also as 'the cat from the Blue Nile', Aby is affectionate, medium sized and short haired.

Behaviour problems in cats are usually the result of a badly-behaved owner. If you don't provide a scratching post your cat is going to use the nearest chair or carpet on which to sharpen her nails. If she does particularly bad things like walking through your fried eggs or spraying the lasagna, she is probably trying to punish you for ignoring her.

Devon Rexes enjoy living in apartments and are generally good-tempered fellows. Their appearance is a little weird; they have very large ears, curly hair and crinkly skins but they are much loved and prove the point that beauty is only skin deep.

Fat cats are at their fattest in Australia, where 'Edward Bear' from New South Wales weighed in at 21.7kg and 'Himmy' from Queensland died, aged ten, weighing 21.3kg. According to *The Guinness Book of Records*, Britain's fattest cat is 'Poppa', who weighed 20.19kg at the age of eleven.

Gumbie Cats

'I have a Gumbie Cat in
mind, her name is
Jennyanydots;
Her coat is of the tabby kind,
with tiger stripes and leopard
spots.
All day she sits upon the stair or
on the steps or on the mat:
She sits and sits and sits and sits –
and that's what makes a
Gumbie Cat!'

Old Possum's Book of Practical Cats,
T.S. Eliot

Himalayan or Colourpoint

Long-hairs are taking over
the world faster than any
other breed of cat. This isn't sur-
prising, because a Persian coat in
Siamese colours is smart by any
standard. If you put this coat on a
good-tempered and placid darling
with a highly developed sense of
curiosity, what Tom could resist.

Interesting Cats:

'There are no
ordinary cats,' wrote Colette.
She also wrote, 'it is the animal
to whom the Creator gave the
biggest eye, the softest fur, the
most supremely delicate nostrils, a
mobile ear, an unrivalled paw, a
curved claw borrowed from the
rose tree...'

Jellicle Cats

'Jellicle Cats are black and
white,
Jellicle Cats are rather small,
Jellicle Cats are merry and bright,
And pleasant to hear when they
caterwaul.'

Old Possum's Book of Practical Cats,
T.S. Eliot

Kissing Cats:

Muslim legend
says that the cat was born
of a bizarre love affair
between a beautiful lioness and a
monkey. Cats, of course, kiss by
sniffing noses.

Longlife Cats:

Devon, England
is a place where cats have
been known to survive to a
great old age. One particular tabby
was laid to rest aged 34 years and
another, from the same county,
died on November 28th, 1939 aged
36, one day after his birthday.

Manx or 'Rumpy' cats

are
surrounded by legend.
Some say they are a cross
between a cat and a rabbit, others
that the Manx lost its tail when
Noah closed the door of the Ark on
it. However the tail was lost, the
Manx arrived on the Isle of Man in
the sixteenth century, supposedly
swimming there as survivor of a
wrecked Spanish galleon. A true
Manx has no tail at all, not even a
stump.

Name that Cat:

Words for
'cat' are very similar the
world over and are based
on sound or action: in Arabic,
Basque, German and Greek we
have *kittah*, *catua*, *katze* and *kata*. In
Chinese and Egyptian we have *miu*
and *mau* and in Italian, Polish,
Portuguese and Spanish we have
gatto, *gatto*, *gato* and *gato*... I won-
der if that is why they love cream?

'Orrible Cats:

Those who
hate cats are ailuro-
phobes and the most
celebrated in history was
Napoleon. According to popular
legend, an aide-de-camp was pass-
ing the door of his bedroom when
he heard his Emperor calling for
help.

'Opening the door hastily, and
rushing into the room, he saw the

greatest soldier of the age, half undressed, his countenance agitated, beaded drops of perspiration standing on his brow, making frequent and convulsive lunges with his sword through the tapestry that lined the walls, behind which a cat had secreted herself. Madame Junot was aware of this weakness and is reported to have gained an important political advantage over the Little Corporal merely by mentioning a cat at the right moment.'

Tiger in the House,
Carl van Vechten, 1921

Hitler was another ailurophobe.

Peke-Face Persian is quite a contradiction in terms but the breed was developed in the United States during the thirties from the Standard Red and Red Tabby Persians. The idea is that their features resemble those of a Pekinese dog with a flat face, large round eyes and prominent ears. As a result, these cats often have deformed teeth and lower jaws which makes breathing difficult. Personally I think a Poodle-Face Persian would be a much better proposition.

'Queen' is the term used for a female cat. To sex a kitten, lift its tail: males have two round openings, the anus and, beneath it, the tip of the penis; the female has two 'i'-shaped openings, the vertical slit below being the vulva and the 'dot' above it the anus. You cannot see the testicles on male kittens so don't be misled when you don't find them.

Ragdolls are very gentle, floppy cats who need a great deal of attention because of their lack of fear. They often wear white boots and mittens and should be kept away from other animals and children who might harm them.

Socks the Cat worked hard to achieve presidential status for Clinton, so hard in fact that a nervous breakdown followed. Plagued by the press, Socks withdrew from public life and left political matters in the safe hands of Hillary, President-in-waiting.

Tom-cat

'At midnight in the alley
A Tom-cat comes to wail,
And he chants the hate of a million
    years
As he swings his snaky tail.

Malevolent, bony, brindled,
Tiger and devil and bard,
His eyes are coals fron the middle
    of Hell
And his heart is black and hard.

He twists and crouches and capers
And bares his curved sharp claws,
And he sings to the stars of the jun-
    gle nights
Ere cities were, or laws.

Beast from a world primeval,
He and his leaping clan,
When the blotched red moon leers
    over the roofs
Give voice to their scorn of man

He will lie on a rug tomorrow
And lick his silky fur,
And veil the brute in his yellow
    eyes
And play he's tame and purr.

Don Marquis

Unusually kind cat: 'One evening, as the family were seated round the fire, they observed a mouse make its way from the cupboard, which was near the fireplace, and lay itself down on the stomach of the cat, as a kitten would do when she is going to suck. Surprised at what they saw, and afraid of disturbing the mouse, which appeared to be full grown, they did not immediately ascertain whether it was in the act of sucking or not. After remaining with the cat a considerable length of time, it returned to the cupboard. These visits were repeated on several other occasions and were witnessed by many persons. The cat not only appeared to accept the mouse, but uttered that sort of greeting purr which the animal is so well known to make use of when she is visited by her kitten.'

Our Dumb Companions,
Revd T. Jackson, c.1863

Value was placed on cats in around 945 AD by the Welsh king Hywel Dda (Howell the Good). He passed a series of laws aimed at protecting the cat and establishing its value for compensation if killed or stolen. This was related to 'mousing' ability: 'The price of a kitten before it can see is one penny. If it has caught a mouse, its value is raised to twopence, and afterwards to fourpence. If anyone should steal or slay the cat guarding the royal granary, he shall be compelled either to forfeit an ewe or as much wheat as will cover the cat when suspended by its tail.'

The Secret Life of Cats,
Robert de Laroche

Working cats can be found in all walks of life: down on the farm protecting foodstuffs and at 10 Downing Street (the British Prime Minister's residence) on mouse patrol. Ships' cats were considered important enough to have their own signal, five minutes before departure, calling them to return to ship, and cats throughout the world have received financial support in exchange for mousing, guarding and, of course, advertising.

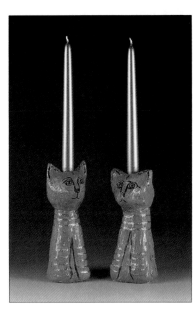

Your cat, be she a thorough-bred or a moggy, will, if treated with care and kind-ness, prove a true friend and com-panion. Always remember that she is an individual with her own needs – she will doubtless make those known to you early on in the relationship. The cat is historically a symbol of Liberty, Femininity and Maternity. She is a moonchild who has been feared and wor-shipped in equal measure. In fact, for a small four-legged furry little creature she has certainly made an enormous impact on our lives.

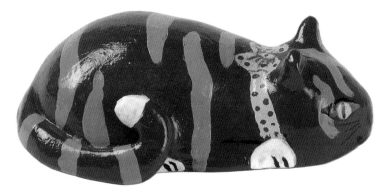

Xquisite cats: All cats are exquisite but the most trea-sured of all breeds has to be the Siamese. It is suggested that Siamese cats originated in the Royal Palace in Siam (Thailand) where the king employed them as palace guards. In addition to their elegant and aristo-cat-ic appear-ance, they are blessed with an intelligent and playful personality. Because of their royal origins they tend to be somewhat demanding and self-centred, but they are extremely affectionate, sing well and can be taken for walks on a lead.

Zee End

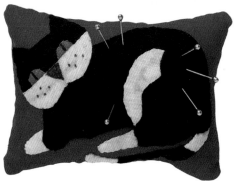

How to Draw a Cat

To draw a cat's head, start with a squashed circle, like this:

Then add two smaller circles for the snout, and pencil in a vertical and horizontal cross to add dimension, like this:

Use those lines as a guide for positioning the ears, eyes, nose and mouth:

Then add the detail and rub out the lines:

In profile, work in a similar fashion, i.e. draw a circle, and add a snout:

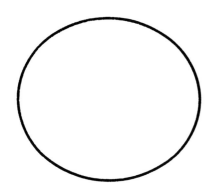

Draw in lines to show dimensions and position for features:

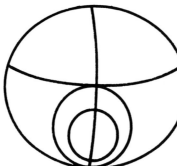

You can play around with the position of the snout to have the cat looking up or down and you can move the pupils or re-shape the eyes to create different expressions.

Fill in the detail:

The cat's body can be broken down in a similar fashion. Draw a cylinder for the body then add the head and neck, the rear quarters, tail, shoulders and legs.

Note the wide hind quarters and the leg joints, and also the position where the legs join the body. The cat's expression and movement can be changed by the slant of the ears, but body movements are always fluid and sleek. Build your design up gradually in pencil until you are happy with the proportions and then fill in the detail like this:

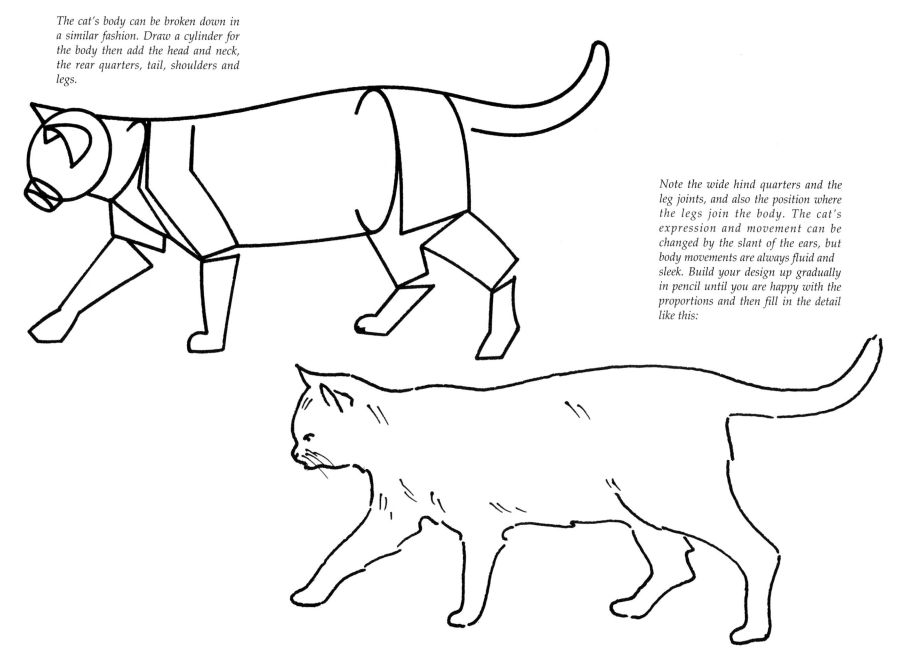

Doughcraft and Modelling

or how to squidge a cat

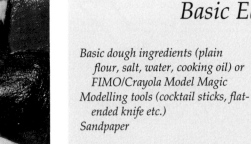

Basic Equipment

*Basic dough ingredients (plain
    flour, salt, water, cooking oil) or
    FIMO/Crayola Model Magic
Modelling tools (cocktail sticks, flat-
    ended knife etc.)
Sandpaper*

*Water-based paints
Paintbrushes
Polyurethane varnish
Cotton rags
White spirit*

If you have always wanted to try making pottery but don't have a kiln, experiment with these modelling techniques.

Doughcraft is easy and great fun for all the family and you will be surprised at how easy it is to make a huge variety of different things. The dough can be dried in a normal oven to a rock-hard finish or, on a warm day, you can even dry it in the sun. The finished pieces can be coloured with water-based paints or felt-tipped pens and, with a coat of varnish, your creation will have a professional long-lasting finish that will look like pottery.

For those who cannot be bothered with dough, all of the fol-lowing projects can be produced with FIMO, a 'household' clay that can be oven-dried and painted. FIMO is available in a number of colours in addition to white so you can get some very clever results without even touching a paintbrush. Another revolution-ary addition to modelling compounds is Crayola Model Magic. It feels like marshmallow and it air-dries overnight, retaining a slightly rubbery finish. It is light, which makes it perfect for sending through the post, doesn't stick to fingers or clothes and can be painted in the normal way with water-based paints. I love it.

Dough recipe

To make around 20 small cats (halve or quarter my quantities if you want to make less):

2 cups (8oz/225g) plain flour
1 cup (4oz/100g) salt
1 cup water
1 tbs cooking oil

Mix all the above ingredients together and knead until they have a soft, smooth consistency. If the dough is too dry, add a little oil; if too gritty, knead it some more, as the salt hasn't been properly absorbed.

All the projects in this book are made up either with balls of dough in various sizes, rolled round and round on a table until smooth, or with 'snakes' of dough, rolled into tubes with the palm of the hand then cut into various lengths. Pieces are joined together by wetting and pressing gently into position, and features can be added with a sharp cocktail stick or knitting needle. For 'fur', try pressing a ball of dough through a garlic crusher, and for badges in various shapes and sizes you can use pre-shaped pastry cutters, bottle tops or whatever comes to hand in the shape you want to achieve.

When you have completed your perfect piece, put it in the oven at the very lowest setting and leave it for around six hours. Alternatively, leave your tray of finished items in an airing cupboard or similar warm place until

it is completely dry. To test it for dryness, try pushing a needle into it: this should not be possible.

Troubleshooting

If bits fall off during the drying process you can glue them on again.

If the dough cracks during baking the oven is too high. Lower the temperature of the oven and stick the figure together again by wetting the bits that should join each other and pressing them into place.

Dingle and Dangle

To make these FIMO earrings you will need:

A small block of white FIMO
Orange, green and black paint
Earring attachments

Most good craft shops sell a selection of attachments for earrings and they can also be bought by mail order (see Stockist Information, p.89).

To make these earrings, work the FIMO between your fingers until it is soft and then roll out two thin sausages approximately 3in (8cm) in length. Fold these in half to form an upside-down U shape. Turn the bottoms up to form feet. Roll two small balls of FIMO and pinch out ears. Press these into position at the top left of your upside-down U. Roll a very thin sausage and press on for tail, curling it over the back leg. Push ear

ring attachment firmly into the top centre of the U. Follow the manufacturer's drying instructions. When dry and hard, paint all over with orange paint. Leave to dry then add paws, ears and body stripes in green. Dot on eyes, nose and mouth with black paint and a very fine brush. When dry, add two coats of varnish, glue onto earring attachments, attach to ears and go out on the tiles.

Catacomb

Dress up a pair of plain plastic haircombs with these two prima-donnas.

You will need:

White FIMO
Haircombs
Paint in orange, grey, green and black
*   or colours of your choice*
UHU glue

To make the ginger cat, roll out a 2in (5cm) sausage for the body and a 1½in (4cm) sausage for the tail. Fold the body piece into an upside-down U, then roll a ball for the head and flatten it. Pinch out ear shapes, and press onto body piece. Flatten the end of the tail piece and curve it around the comb. Take it off the comb, being careful to keep the shape, and dry following the manufacturer's instructions.

When completely dry, glue the body/head to the front of the comb and the tail into position on the back. When the glue is dry, paint in colourings and markings as indicated on the photograph. When paint is dry, add two coats of varnish.

The grey tabby is made in the same way except for the body shape. To make the body, roll out a sausage 1½in (4cm) thick and flat-ten. Add two 1in (2½cm) sausages for the legs and a 1½in (4cm) sausage for the tail and press into place. Make the head from a flat-tened ball with the ears pinched out. Press into position. Continue as for the ginger cat but glue the cat onto the front of your comb.

Purr-fect Image

To make this doughcraft mirror, in addition to the basic materials you will need:

Dough (see recipe, p.9)
A mirror measuring
  4½in x 5½in (11cm x 14cm)
An A4 sheet of waxed paper
An A4 sheet of lightweight card
  (a cereal box would do)
Paints in brown, tan, pink, white,
  black, yellow or colours of your
  choice
UHU glue
A non-stick baking sheet

First, take the card and draw onto it a rectangle 7in x 11in (17½cm x 27½cm). With a ruler, mark off every 1in (2½cm) on all four sides of the rectangle, then join up these points to form a grid of 1in (2½cm) squares. Turn to the template on p.77 and copy the shape onto your grid, square by square. Then trace off the cat shape you have copied and transfer onto the waxed paper.

Cut the shape from the waxed paper (including the hole for the mirror) and cut the outline shape only from the card. Lay the card to one side and place the waxed paper cutout onto your baking sheet, waxed side up.

Using the cutout as a guide, form the body shape by rolling a thick sausage circle of dough and pressing it onto the waxed cutout. The dough should be about ¾ in (2 cm) thick. Form the head and ear shapes and press firmly onto the body, overlapping the dough to prevent a weak join. Make a hole in the centre of the head large enough for a nail. Form a bow from dough and press over the head/body join. Roll and flatten four balls of dough for the paws, adding small flattened balls for the paw pads and nose. Make a sausage for the tail, curling it over the left top paw.

Bake overnight at the lowest setting on your oven or until completely dry.

Meanwhile, position the mirror on your card cutout and glue down firmly right side up. When the dough is dry, rub over gently with fine sandpaper to obtain a smooth finish. Glue the dough cat over the mirrored card, making a nail hole in the card to match the position of the one already in the dough. Paint as required and, when dry, apply two coats of varnish.

Paper Tiger

You can make lots of small, simple items from your left-over dough, including this paperweight, which is an ideal project for a child.

Roll a ball of dough to the shape and size of a large egg. Roll another ball for the head and pinch out ears. Press onto one end of the egg shape. Make a sausage for the tail and press into position. Bake at the lowest setting on your oven overnight or until completely dry. Rub with sandpaper for a smooth finish and paint the whole piece brown. Leave the paint to dry and add tan stripes for facial features, white paws and tail tip, and a colourful neck bow.

When paint is dry, add two coats of varnish.

Spot that Cat

Badges are great fun and can be simply made from a flattened ball of dough with a safety pin or brooch clip glued firmly to the back. When the badge shape is cooked, paint on a base colour and, when dry, draw on a cat head outline with a felt-tipped pen. Then fill in the colours with water-based paints and a fine paintbrush.

You could use special effect pens to give a glittery collar or, if you do not feel confident about drawing your own cat freehand, you could glue a magazine cutout of a cat onto the dough and varnish over the top. You could of course cut out cat-shaped badges using a biscuit cutter or by tracing off one of the smaller templates at the back of this book. You could even glue a small photo of your favourite cat onto the disc and glue an outline circle of dough over the top to form a frame. If you make a hole in the top centre of the disc, you could wear your finished masterpiece as a necklace or add earring attachments for big dangly earrings.

Be sure to put two coats of varnish on your finished work to add strength.

Cat Plaque

This fun cat plaque is simple to make and looks very pretty hung on the wall. To make him useful as well as decorative, press in a couple of small hooks along the bottom and hang your keys from him.

In addition to the basic materials, you will need:

Dough (see recipe, p.9)
Water-based paints in black, white, red, blue, pink and yellow
A rolling pin

Roll out an oblong of dough measuring approximately 6in x 4in (15cm x 10cm) and ½in (1cm) thick. Roll out a ½in (1cm) sausage, long enough to fit right around the edge, and press into position. Mark the sausage every ¼in (½cm) to form a decorative frame. Make an egg shape of dough and flatten it onto the centre of the plaque to form the body. Roll and flatten a ball of dough to form the head and add two small triangles for the ears. Add two small flattened circles for the cheeks and a small ball for the nose. Press on four 2in (5cm) sausages for the legs and a thin sausage for the tail. Make a hole with a cocktail stick or matchstick in the centre top of the plaque to hold a nail, and press in key hooks if required.

Bake overnight at the lowest setting on your oven or until completely dry, then rub over gently with fine sandpaper until smooth. Paint in the white details first and leave to dry. Add the nose, eyes and mouth. Paint in the black body and head, and finally the background and frame. If the dough has not secured the key hooks properly, glue them in place when the dough is dry. When finished, paint on two coats of varnish.

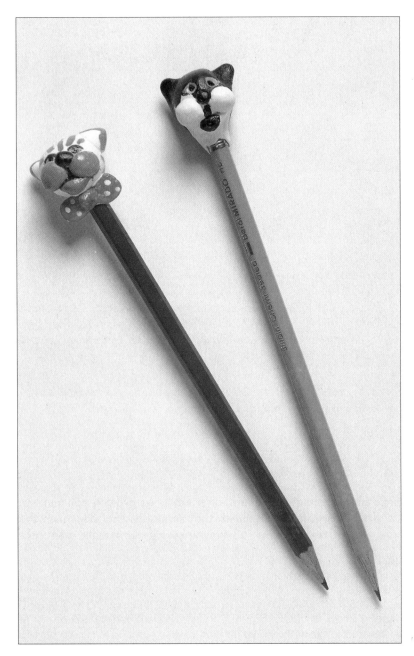

Top of his Class

You will need:

Crayola Model Magic
Pencils
Water-based paints in pink, black,
green, blue, white and yellow, or
colours of your choice

To make these simple pencil tops, roll a ball of Crayola Model Magic and press it onto the top of your pencil. Add two small balls (shaped into triangles) for the ears, then press on two small balls side by side for the cheeks, positioning them in the middle of the head. Add one for the nose where the cheeks join together and one for the chin, directly below the cheeks. Press a 1in (2½ cm) flattened sausage under the chin to form a bow, with a small ball in the middle for the knot.

Leave to dry overnight and then paint the cheeks, chin, head and ear stripes in pink. When the pink is dry, paint the nose black and fill in where the cheeks and chin join with a line of black for the mouth. The eyes are painted as half circles either side of the nose and directly above the cheeks. Fill in the eyes with green paint and paint the bow in blue, leaving white spots showing through. Varnish.

Use the same method to make the black and white cat, but leave out the bow and position the cat head so that a bit of the original gold pencil top can be seen, giving the impression of a collar. Make the eyes with a matchstick and fill in the holes with colour.

The above method has also been used to make the head for 'Mummy Cat' in the 'Pot-Purr-i Family' on p.32.

Mashed Cats

Papier mâché is a cheap, fun, rewarding pastime that can produce some stunningly decorative results. It also helps the environment by using up those piles of newspaper that might otherwise be burnt.

There are several approaches to this craft, each giving different results; the various techniques are described next to the projects they were used for.

Papier mâché can be scrunched, sanded or shredded to create different finishes. You can add layers and layers to give the effect of china or stone, or you can leave the finish rough to give the impression of fur. With the addition of several coats of varnish you can ensure that the finished item will be hard-wearing and you can use your painting skills to present your cat in a suitable light, taking into account, of course, how extremely fussy he is about his appearance.

In producing this section I solicited the help of a wonderful cat artist: Paula Murray has been making cats for a number of years and it is sometimes difficult to distinguish between her masterpieces and the real thing. However, if you follow her basic instructions and put some time and care into your project, you too can achieve the professional finish that separates the men from the moggies. My neighbour, Judy Newman, also tried her skills and produced the candlesticks on p.24.

Do not limit yourself to the items I have made. Start with something easy like the 'Dishy Cat' on p.16 and progress to the more difficult projects when you have more confidence. Once you feel happy with the results you can make your own bowls, vases, egg-cups and ornaments. I guarantee there will be no stopping you.

Basic Equipment

Newspaper
Wallpaper paste
A paste bowl
Balloons, plasticine or moulds
Petroleum jelly
Sellotape
Sandpaper
Copydex glue
An old, blunt kitchen knife

Scissors
Pencils
Water-based paints including white
    emulsion
Paintbrushes
Polyurethane varnish
Cotton rags
White spirit

Dishy Cat

This is a very simple project to start off with. In addition to the basics you will need:

A dish (any simple shape will do) to use as a mould
Paints in white, green and black
A jar of water for washing out brushes

To make this dish, tear a newspaper into 3–4in (7–10cm) squares and mix up a bowl of wallpaper paste according to the manufacturer's instructions. If you put the made-up paste into an airtight container it will keep for about a week.

Take the dish and cover it liberally with petroleum jelly. Dip the pieces of paper into your paste and squeeze off the excess with your fingers.

Place the pasted paper on the greased dish piece by piece to form one complete layer. Smooth out air bubbles or creases with your fingers and leave for 24 hours to dry. Repeat the above process until you have completed four layers of paper.

When the last layer is dry, gently lift the papier mâché layer from the dish. You might need a blunt kitchen knife to lever the edges off. Trim off any excess paper around the edges with a pair of scissors. If you see any lumps and bumps, gently remove these with sandpaper.

Paint the whole dish with white emulsion and, when it is completely dry, trace off the template on p.77 onto your dish with a pencil. Paint the whole area outside your tracing with two coats of green paint (I have used Deka-Lac, a water-based, high-gloss enamel). When these are dry, carefully outline the cat and his facial features in black paint, using a fine brush. Leave to dry, then apply two coats of varnish.

Russian Cats

These stacking cats are perennial favourites and easy to make. For moulds I used plasticine lumps, coated in petroleum jelly, in progressively larger sizes. A word of warning, however: make sure that the base of the cat is the widest point or you could have a problem getting the plasticine out. If you do find it difficult to remove the plasticine, slit the dried papier mâché shape from top to bottom down the centre back and, when you have removed the mould, add another layer of paper.

To make the cats, use the same method as for the dish opposite. Once they are completed and coated with white emulsion, draw on the facial features with a pencil and, when you are happy with them, paint in the detail using the pencil marks as a guideline. You can then add cat markings of your choice to the surrounding areas. Leave to dry, then apply two coats of varnish.

Cat a List

This handy note pad is purrfect for recording cat calls and easier to make than it looks. There is a template for the shape in the back of the book. Get the message?

You will need, in addition to the basic equipment:

*An A4 sheet of medium-weight card-
  board*
Toilet tissue
*A block of 3in (8cm) square 'Post It'
  notelets*
A pen
*Paints in ochre, white, pink, black and
  blue (I have used Deka-Lac water-
  based enamel)*
*A pair of cat's safety eyes measuring
  approx ½in (1cm) (see Stockist
  Information, p.89)*
*3 strands of horsehair or stiff thread
  for whiskers*
A sewing needle

To make this cat, first take the card and draw onto it a rectangle 11in x 8in (27½cm x 20cm). With a ruler, mark off every 1in (2½cm) on all four sides of the rectangle, then join up these points to form a grid of 1in (2½cm) squares. Turn to the template on p.78 and copy the shape onto your grid, square by square.

Cut around the outside shape. Then cover the whole cardboard cat with pasted newspaper and leave to dry. Coat with emulsion and, when dry, paint the area inside the dotted line with one coat of blue paint.

Tear off sheets of toilet tissue and immerse them in wallpaper paste. Squeeze out excess moisture and begin to apply them to the areas outside the dotted line, starting with the feet. Build up the layers of scrunched tissue paper until they are approximately 1in (2½cm) thick, adding extra thicknesses to the paws, cheeks and nose, ear surrounds and forehead. If in doubt, ask your favourite cat to model for you and pad out his finer points.

When this is completely dry, coat the tissue-clad areas in ochre paint, then, with a fine brush and black paint, outline the nose and mouth. When dry, paint in the nose and the centres of the ears in pink. Next, using a 1in (2½cm) brush, paint in stripes, paws, cheeks and chin in white. Finally, add another coat of blue to the centre panel and, when dry, add two coats of varnish to the whole piece.

Push the eyes into position as indicated on the template and, with a long sewing needle, thread whiskers through the cheeks, catching them down with adhesive if they refuse to curl in the right direction.

Glue a note pad to the centre of the plain blue area and push a pen in through the card, just above the cat's right paw.

Cat Mint

This project and the two following ones use a carving technique. Don't panic: remember you are dealing with paper, so the process is more like peeling an apple than carving a lump of wood. If you want to try out your skills before embarking on a major project, take a lump of plasticine and see if you can carve a cat's face into it.

In addition to the basic materials, you will need:

A round balloon
A cork or plastic stopper (maybe off an old spice jar)
A craft knife

To make this cat, coat a part-inflated balloon with petroleum jelly and then cover with strips of torn newspaper pasted on both sides with wallpaper paste. Apply three layers and allow to dry. Add crumpled dry newspaper for the front legs of the cat and attach with sellotape. Crumple a ball of dry newspaper for the head. Now cover the whole shape with pasted strips, making sure you do no more than three layers before allowing it to dry completely in a warm place.
   The shape is created by adding paper pulp, made by kneading pasted paper with the fingertips on a hard surface and carving the detail with a craft knife when dry. Continue adding the pulp, wrap-ping with pasted strips and carving until you are happy with the shape and firmness. * Add a raised rim of paper around the bottom edge, leaving a hollow for the stopper.
   Make a hole at the centre of the hollow by inserting first a craft knife and then a pencil with a piece of medium sandpaper wrapped

(Continued overleaf)

Cat Mint (contd)

Stop that Cat

around it to form a file. File away the papier mâché from the centre outwards until you create a hole that is the correct size for your cork or stopper. Make sure it's big enough to get your money out – cats can be very stingy. Next, cut a slot in the cat's back and paint both these openings with glue to seal the edges.

The ears are made with a strip of pasted paper folded into a square and then a triangle. Curve the triangle in half again, pinching the narrow top to form the ear point and pasting the wider bottom into position on the cat's head. Paste further strips of paper over the ear to secure it firmly to the head and cover the join.

When the cat is dry, sand it thoroughly all over to remove crinkles and loose bits and then paint on a coat of white emulsion. Draw on the eyes, nose, mouth and paws and, when you are happy with the expression, paint over the lines with black paint and a very fine paintbrush. Leaving the white patches white, paint the rest of the cat in black emulsion. For extra detail add small dots of black paint over the white edges to give a furry effect. When the paint is dry, add two coats of varnish.

In case you were wondering, the balloon should have burst by now!

This big tom is designed to hold the kitchen door open to ensure easy access to tins of pilchards. He is made in exactly the same way as 'Cat Mint' (see p.19), so follow those instructions up to *.

In addition to the basic equipment you will need:

A round balloon
A large stone approximately 4in
    (10cm) in diameter
Polyfilla
A pair of yellow ¾in (2cm) safety
    cat's eyes (see Stockist Information,
    p.89)
A craft knife
A small natural sponge

When you are happy with the cat's shape and firmness, take your craft knife and cut him across the back, almost in half. Burst the balloon and insert the stone, wrapped in newspaper. Seal the join with strips of paper and make sure that the underneath of the cat is strong enough to support the weight. If not, you should either use a smaller stone or add extra layers of paper to the bottom.

Make and attach ears as for 'Cat Mint'. Make holes for positioning the eyes and fill with Polyfilla, then press in the eyes being careful to get the angle right. Remove surplus Polyfilla from the surface and leave to dry.

Sand the whole cat thoroughly

to remove crinkles and loose bits and then paint with white emulsion. The markings have been worked by applying layers of shaded colour with a sponge, using a paintbrush for the more solid lines. You can also splatter on

markings by flicking a brush loaded with paint. Make sure that one colour has dried before applying a second, and practise on a plain piece of card before tackling the cat himself. When the paint is dry, add two coats of varnish.

Cat Literate

These cats are made using the same methods as for 'Cat Mint'. The actual structure they sit on is decorated with decoupage (see p.62).

In addition to the basic equipment, you will need the following:

2 egg-sized stones
2 pieces of heavyweight card, each measuring 15in x 5in (38cm x 13cm)
A large sheet of decorative wrapping paper

To make each book end, wrap the stone in dry newspaper. Crumple more paper into a ball for the head and add more crumpled paper as necessary to achieve the body shape, keeping it together with sellotape. Now cover the shape with strips of well pasted newspaper. Continue as for 'Cat Mint' (p.19) but do not make the money slot or the stopper hole. When the cat is complete and thoroughly sanded, paint with white emulsion and decorate as for 'Stop that Cat' (p.20).

To make the base, take your strip of cardboard and fold it to make a 9in (23cm) upright back and a 6in (15cm) flat base. Cover on both sides with about 25 layers of pasted newspaper, allowing it to dry in three-layer stages. (Take care to dry it at a right angle using weights as props.) Sand well, then paste on pieces of decorative wrapping paper. Apply two coats of varnish to give a protective finish.

Cats by Candlelight

These two smart candlesticks have been made from papier mâché, and then coated with plaster of Paris to make them fireproof.

In addition to the basic equipment you will need:

2 cones or cardboard cylinders for base
26oz (750g) plaster of Paris powder

Take a cardboard cylinder (a toilet roll inner would do) or a knitting wool cone and sellotape to it a screwed-up ball of newspaper for the head.

Tear up strips of newspaper and paste them onto the body and head shape in layers, leaving an indentation at the top of the head big enough to take a household candle loosely. Check that the size of the hole remains constant as you build up layers of paper. When you have built up a few layers, add folded triangles for the ears as described in the instructions for 'Cat Mint' (see p.19).

Continue adding layers until you are happy with the shape. Mix a paste from plaster of Paris, following manufacturer's instructions. When the cat is completely dry begin applying plaster with a 1in (2½cm) brush. Apply a total of four coats, leaving each coat to dry for approximately six hours. (After the plaster of Paris application, the finished head should be around the same size as the finished base to ensure a good balance.) When the last coat has dried, paint with white emulsion and then decorate (I have used Deka-Lac water-based enamel paints). Finally, add two coats of varnish.

N.B. Although the plaster of Paris assists in fireproofing your candle-sticks, never tempt providence by leaving candles to burn right down to the end!

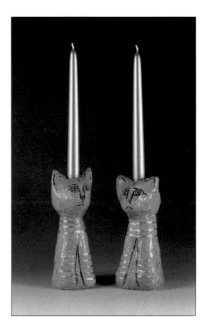

Fabricated Cats

There is really no excuse in this life for throwing things out. This is how I feel and, as a result, nobody comes to visit me because there isn't any room to sit down. But seriously, that first pair of nursery curtains could last you your whole life through – all that is needed is a sharp pair of scissors and a little bit of imagination.

Fabric can be torn into strips and plaited, cut into shapes and patched or cut and pieced together into pussycats of all shapes and sizes. Even when you have finished making the projects in this book you are bound to have some left over. Don't thow it away: use it as stuffing for a very smart cat cushion for puss to rest her weary little head on.

If you can sew then, of course, the world is your oyster; but if you can't, that's no excuse, as you can use glue instead. If you don't like the colour of your fabric, dye it; if you don't like the texture, bead it. There are some wonderful special effect paints available which are perfect for adding the odd whisker or two, and you can also obtain bonding fabric which is great for no-sew appliques. Use your fabric with other mediums such as paper, wood, and even pipe cleaners. Until you try it you will never know your own purr-tential.

Here are a few ideas to start you off.

Basic Equipment

A ragbox of fabric offcuts
Sewing thread to match fabrics used
Sewing needles
Pins

Scissors
An iron and ironing board
A marker pen
Copydex glue

Hooked-on Cat

There are very few cats who allow themselves to be walked on, so this hooked rug could be made especially for feline indoor sunbathing or perhaps hung on the wall. You should have enough materials around the house; if not, you can scour jumble and car boot sales for interesting pieces of clothing to cut up. Wool is the best material to use for hooked and plaited rugs but the only real limitation in selecting your fabrics is wear and tear and aftercare. If you happen to have an aristocat, one would assume she would be happy reclining on velvet and brocade; the average kind of moggy might be better placed on wool.

The old hometown tradition is to give your brand new rug the place of honour in the parlour and then, when it becomes a little 'dog-eared', to move it to the kitchen, then the hallway, finally relegating it to the position of 'doormat'. Rug hooking has always been a communal activity so you can involve all your friends and family – and no doubt Cat will want to help paw through some fabrics too.

In addition to the basic equipment, you will need:

Cotton fabric scraps, weighing
  approximately 4½ lb (2kg) in total.
  We used the following colours:
Cat: tan, mustard, beige and peach
Outline: black

Bag a Cat

Background: green, yellow and blue,
  in plain and printed fabric
Fringe: green and black

A rug hook (an open-ended steel hook
  set in a wooden handle; see
  Stockist Information, p.89).
  N.B. A latchhook won't work.
A frame 34in x 22in (87cm x 56cm)
  This can be made very simply by
  nailing 4 lengths of 2in x 1in
  (5cm x 2½cm) wood together to form
  a square. Hammer flat pieces of
  wood diagonally across the corners
  to make it sturdy.
2 pieces of hessian, one 34in x 22in
  (87cm x 56cm), the other 36in
  x 24in (89½cm x 58½cm)
A sheet of A3 paper
Nails or carpet tacks

To make the rug it is advisable to work on a frame. However, if you are going to insist on scrunching the whole thing up on your lap, do be careful that you don't have any four-legged friends helping you, as you could mistakenly hook through the odd tail thinking it is a length of fabric.

Once you have knocked together a frame, stretch the smaller piece of hessian over it, tacking it down first at the four corners and then approximately every ½in (1cm). The hessian should now be taut.

In the centre of the framed hessian, draw a rectangle 15in x 9in (37½cm x 22½cm) with black felt-tipped pen. Then mark off every 1in (2½cm) on all four sides of the rectangle, and join up these points to form a grid of 1in (2½cm) squares. Turn to the template on p.78 and copy the shape onto your grid, square by square. At this stage you should draw on the cat's markings: stripes, splodges or whatever you fancy.

It is a good idea to work all the outlines first and then select fabrics to fill in. The background is made up of a series of wavy lines criss-crossing over each other and worked with different coloured fabrics. You might want to work the cat before tackling the background; alternatively you could draw in the wavy lines now but leave a 6in (15cm) border of hessian free for fringing and hemming.

The fabric should be cut or torn into strips (as long as you can make them) measuring ¾in (2cm) in width. The raw edges should be folded into the centre and pressed flat to avoid fraying. Begin by outlining the cat in black fabric. Choose a rag strip and, with your left hand, hold the strip behind the frame. With your right hand, insert the hook through the front of the hessian, pick up the strip with the hook and pull it through to the front, making a small but firm loop. Skip a few threads, then push the hook in again from front to back and pull through the next loop. The loops should be as close together as possible, following the line of the design. When you reach the end of the strip of fabric, pull it through to the front and trim it to the length of the loops. Do not cut the loops.

When you have completed your design and the background it is time to add the fringe. Cut strips of fabric measuring 1½in x 6in (4cm x 15cm), fold in half lengthways and cut diagonally across the double thickness so each end is pointed. Then hook both ends through the hessian, leaving them free and working the strips closely together. Work to a depth of 4in (10cm) and fold the remaining border back on itself to form a double hem. Stitch down.

For neatness it is a good idea to back your rug with a second piece of hessian, folded in at the edges and stitched into position around the outside of the completed piece.

Here is a nifty way of taking your cat shopping with you. Hook a portrait of your favourite cat onto a square of hessian, back it with another square, add a handle and voilà!

In addition to the basic equipment you will need:

A piece of hessian sacking, 20in
  (50cm) square
A wooden frame, 18in (47cm) square
Nails or carpet tacks
Marker pen
Around 10in (25cm) of each of the
  following coloured fabrics (I used
  cottons): purple, mauve, cream,
  white, yellow, peach, dark green,
  bright green, black, red, blue
Around 1 yard (1 metre) of fabric for

(Continued overleaf)

Bag a Cat (contd.)

the background (I cut up a pair of tan leggings)
2 pieces of backing fabric, each 24in (60cm) square (I used red hessian)
Another piece of the same fabric, 45in x 5in (114cm x 13cm)
A wooden frame, 18in (47cm) square (see instructions for 'Hooked-on Cat', p.26)
A rug hook (see instructions for 'Hooked-on Cat', p.26)
Heavy-duty hessian-coloured cotton thread (or use normal cotton double)
A ruler
A knitting needle
A sewing machine

To make the bag, first stretch the hessian sacking over your frame and tack into place.

With a marker pen, draw a 17in (42½cm) square onto the hessian. Mark off every 1in (2½cm) on all four sides of the square, then join up these points to form a grid of 1in (2½cm) squares. Turn to the template on p.79 and copy the design onto the hessian square by square. Using the colour key, begin hooking (following instructions for 'Hooked-on Cat', p.26), working the cat and flowers first and finishing with the background.

Remove from frame. Turn back raw hessian edges and either stitch or glue them down securely.

Take one square of the red hessian or backing material of your choice and fold in a ¾in (2cm) border at each edge. Press down with an iron.

Centre the finished panel onto the square of backing material and stitch into position, preferably with a machine. The backing material forms a frame around the panel. Fold in the edges of the second piece of backing material in the same way and stitch down. This piece forms the back. Join the back and front along the side and bottom edges. Fold the remaining strip of backing material in half and machine up the seam. Push it through to the right side using a knitting needle or similar. Sew securely to side seams of bag.

Plait-a-Cat Mat

Plaiting is another way of creating a rug cheaply and easily. Once again you can use a selection of fabric oddments. This rug was made with plain and printed cottons with some velvet plaited in for good measure. The black cats have been cut from felt and stitched on when the rug was complete. Alternatively you could apply them with a fabric adhesive such as Copydex.

In addition to the basic equipment, you will need:

2¾lb (1¼kg) cotton and velvet fabrics
8 pieces of black felt, each 12in (31cm)
  square
An A3 piece of card
White tailor's chalk

To make this rug, select, cut and press your fabrics as for 'Hooked-on Cat' (see p.26).

It is a good idea to stitch the lengths together to form strips measuring approximately 5ft (150cm) or long enough to complete an area of colour. Take three strips and knot the ends together. This will form the centre of your rug. Plait them together evenly until your strips are used up, then stitch new lengths onto the ends in colours of your choice. When you have a good length of plaiting you can begin stitching the plait edge to edge into a circle, taking care to keep it flat. Continue in this way

until your circle measures approximately 37in (94cm) in diameter. Fold in and stitch the final ends securely to the rug.

Take the sheet of card and draw onto it a rectangle 12in x 9in (30cm x 22½cm). With a ruler, mark off every 1in (2½cm) on all four sides of the rectangle, then join up these points to form a grid of 1in (2½cm) squares. Turn to the template on p.76 and copy the cat shape onto your grid, square by square, making sure that you copy the 'Plait-a-Cat-Mat' tail. Cut around the shape. Lay the shape onto a square of black felt and outline with tailor's chalk.

Cut out the image. Repeat until you have eight cat silhouettes. Pin the cats into position around the rug, overlapping the tail ends. Stitch neatly into position with small, straight stitches, or glue down with a fabric glue.

You may find that your rug curls up in the middle when you first lay it on the floor. It can be flattened quite easily by treading it down, rolling on it or inviting 24 cats to afternoon tea in front of the fire.

Casbah
and his Wife

Casbah cat is a very exotic character who spends most of his time at his London-based publishers. His wife Cassandra prefers life in the country but both share a taste for quality and comfort. Casbah comes from a well-bred family who purchased his coat from Liberty of London. He married slightly beneath himself, since Cassandra's coat originated from an offcut box somewhere in Wales.

Both coats are made from upholstery-weight cottons suitable for all climates.

To make Casbah or his wife you will need:

Various offcuts of heavyweight cotton fabric or one piece measuring 36in (91cm) square
A piece of dark grey felt, 6in (15cm) square
A piece of peach-coloured felt, 6in (15cm) square
Polyester stuffing
2 large black beads or buttons (use cutouts of black felt or safety eyes if you are making this for a child)
Oddment of black wool and white wool
A strip of corrugated card for collar
Paint in colours of your choice
A jewel for collar (optional)
A sewing machine
A knitting needle

To make Casbah, first trace off the template on p.80 and have it enlarged to A3 at your local copy shop. Then carefully trace off and cut out the pieces as follows. (When cutting through two thicknesses, make sure that the second shape is reversed.)

Fold fabric in half and cut body shape once through two thicknesses. Lay body gusset against fold as indicated and cut once through two thicknesses. Cut one tail piece. Cut one head gusset. Cut eight legs (four through two thicknesses). Cut two ears through two thicknesses. Cut one head through two thicknesses. From grey felt, cut four paws. From peach felt, cut four large pads and sixteen small pads.

Working on the wrong side of the fabric, take the two body pieces and the body gusset and pin the gusset into position matching points A and C. Machine into place, then join back pieces from points B to C (A to B should remain open).

Take the two head pieces and the head gusset and pin the gusset into position on both sides, matching points C and A. Join head from C to B leaving A to B open. Stuff body and head and handstitch open edge of head to open edge of body, adding stuffing to the neck area as you go to make it firm.

Place ear pieces right side together and machine around edge from A to B. Turn the right way out and make a machine line from A to B to form a raised edge. Handstitch ears to head in position marked on head gusset with dotted line.

Place two leg pieces right sides together and machine all around the outer edge from A to B, leaving bottom open. Turn the right side out and stuff. Repeat for other legs. Carefully stitch paws to bottom of legs and glue on one large and four small paw pads. Stitch top edges of legs to body in positions indicated by dotted lines.

Fold tailpiece in half lengthwise, right sides together, and machine stich from A to B. Push through to right side with a knitting needle and lightly stuff bottom half. Handstitch to body.

With black wool, embroider a triangle for the nose at the point where the gusset meets the head shape, and a straight line down the front seam with a mouth at the bottom. Firmly sew on beads or buttons for eyes or cut out circles of black felt and stick these on. With a needle, thread three strands of black or white wool through the face for whiskers and knot near the fabric to prevent them slipping through.

To make a collar, cut a ½in (1cm) strip of corrugated card to fit around the neck with a ½in (1cm) overlap. Paint to required colours and glue around neck, adding a jewel at the front if required.

Cat-ch

These cats are made for juggling and have been filled with barley. However, if you really want to torment your feline you could add some catnip or fill them with pot pourri and leave them lying around the house. If you plan to do this, make sure you machine stitch the pieces very firmly together.

You will need:

Oddments of fabric (You can use woollen, cord, brushed cotton or velvet fabrics. Whatever you choose, make sure it is slightly stretchy, i.e. don't use cotton.)
½lb (225g) of wheat or barley

To make these cats, first trace off the templates on p.84 and mark up your fabric.

Cut out the pieces as indicated on the pattern. Place the two body pieces right sides together and machine or handstitch around them, approximately ½in (1cm) in from the edge, leaving a 2in (5cm) opening at the bottom. Turn the right way out, fill with barley and stitch up the opening.

Take an ear piece and fold it from corner to corner, right sides together, to form a triangle. Stitch together one side, turn it the right way out and fold it in half again with the open side forming the bottom. Tuck in raw edges and stitch to the head in a V shape (separating the front and back slightly at

the base). Repeat for other ear.

Take a leg piece, turn one edge in on itself and from the other edge roll the material into a sausage. Sew down the folded edge, then push in and sew up the bottom edge. Repeat for the other three legs and stitch firmly into position on each side of the body. Do the same with the tail.

The Pot-Purr-i Family

I really enjoyed making this cat family because it was so simple and effective. Mum is sitting on a muslin bag full of lavender but you could use any pot-pourri you like. Apart from one row of running stitch at the top of the skirt, no sewing is involved and you can dress the cats in whatever fabric you choose to suit the mood of the day.

You will need:

Crayola Model Magic (see Stockist Information, p.89)
Water-based paint (I have used Deka-Lac water-based enamels)
Oddments of fabric and lace trims
A piece of muslin, 8in (20cm) square
Pot-pourri
An oddment of raffia

To make the mother cat, take a piece of Model Magic and roll it into a sausage measuring approximately 1in (2½cm) in diameter and 1½in (4cm) in length. Roll out another piece half the diameter and 4in (10cm) in length and push the centre of this onto the top of the first sausage to form a T shape. This forms the cat's body and arms. Bend up the ends of the arms to form paws and push down either side of the centre to form shoulders.

The head is made from one large ball for the main piece with two smaller balls for the cheeks and a tiny ball for the nose. Add small triangles for ears and press completed head onto top of body/shoulders.

Make the head and body for the dressed kitten in the same way, scaling down the size. The baby kitten is made from a 2in (5cm) sausage of Crayola with the ends joined to form a doughnut ring. A ball with the ears pinched out makes the head. Press this onto the centre of the doughnut.

Set the heads and bodies aside to dry overnight. They will dry to a flexible finish which you should then paint in colours of your own choice.

For Mum's dress, cut a strip of fabric measuring 10in x 2½in (25cm x 6cm) and stitch a row of running stitches along one long edge. Place this around her waist, pull the thread to gather the fabric and join at the back when it fits snugly. Wrap and glue a small piece of fabric around each arm to form sleeves and then take a 5in (12½ cm) length of 1in (2½cm)-wide lacy trim and wrap it around her shoulders to form a collar. Glue the ends down at the front.

The hat is made from three lengths of raffia plaited together. Leaving a hole in the centre big enough to sit over the ears, form a continuous circle with the raffia plaits, stitching or gluing each row together as you go until you are happy with the size of the brim. The basket should be made in the same way, but ensure that the top is wide enough to carry the kitten. The handle is a single plait stitched each side of the basket and knotted at the ends.

The dressed kitten's outfit is made in the same way as her mum's, using smaller pieces of fabric.

Next, fill the centre of the muslin square with pot-pourri, pull all the edges of the muslin together to form a bag and secure firmly with cotton. Sit Mother cat on the muslin bag and attach the dressed kitten's paw to her skirt with Copydex. Finally, put baby kitten in her basket.

Peggy's Wedding

Cats are not known for their fidelity, in fact they can be downright promiscuous. It's refreshing, therefore, to see Peggy cat off to take her vows with the groom dressed in his sprayproof velvets and Dad wearing a costume that epitomizes his homespun traditional Scots values. Even the mother of the bride is keeping her claws hidden in case they catch on her beautiful brocade gown. All this finery hides very humble beginnings – old-fashioned clothes pegs and a few ends of wide fancy ribbon.

To make this family you will need:

4 old-fashioned wooden clothes pegs
4 pink pipe cleaners
Scraps of felt for the ears
Wide (2–3in/5–7cm) and narrow fancy ribbons or fabric offcuts including tartan and lace (see Stockist Information, p.89)
Ready-made ribbon roses (or make your own from ribbon or paper)
A fine-nibbed black drawing pen
Paints (I have used Deka-Lac water-based enamels)
A fine paintbrush

Begin by painting the faces with a base coat in the colour of your choice. When that is dry, draw on the facial features with a fine pen and then paint in the cat markings in appropriate colours. Cut small triangles of felt and glue these into position at the back of the heads to form ears.

Cut your pipe cleaners into 5in (12cm) lengths and turn back each end ¼in (½cm) to form paws. Lay the pipe cleaner over a length of ¾in (2cm) ribbon, fold the ribbon in half and glue down on itself to form sleeves. Glue the centre of the ribbon-covered pipe cleaner across the back of the peg just below the neck.

For the bride's dress, cut a 3½in (9cm) strip of 2in (5cm)-wide white satin ribbon and glue it around her middle. All glued joins should be at the back. Then cut a 5in (13cm) piece of 2in (5cm) voile ribbon or a piece of white net, run a thread across the top edge to gather it, secure the gather with a knot and glue this into position around Peggy's waist. (If you prefer not to glue you can fold and sew instead.)

Then glue a 5in (13cm) piece of narrow blue ribbon around the waist, crossing it at the back to form a sash. Take scraps of very narrow lace and glue one of these around the neck, crossing at the front to form a collar, and two more around the bottom of the sleeves to form cuffs. Glue a triangle of net to the back of the head to make a veil, then add one ready-made ribbon flower for a head-dress and three for a bouquet.

The groom's trousers are made from a 2in (5cm) length of 2in (5cm) purple velvet ribbon, cut in half lengthwise and glued around the outside of the peg prongs. Glue a ¾in (2cm) strip of white satin around the top of the peg to form a shirt and then tie and glue the red bow around the neck. Finally, he carries a ready-made red ribbon rose because he is a romantic.

The same principles apply to the making of the mother and father of the bride. Mother's dress has two ready-made roses glued to the shoulders and Father's kilt is one length of 1in (2½cm) tartan ribbon wound twice around the body over a plain black satin wrap.

Cats in Stitches

This section is for that cat-egory of people who like to work with a needle and thread, and includes some very eye cat-ching patchwork designed by Roger and Janet Quilter. I have included a couple of needlepoint projects for those who don't have the time to stitch large projects, a bib, which would be great fun for a child to stitch for his/her new baby brother/sister, and a simple pair of knitted child's mittens.

Basic Equipment

Cottons
Needles and pins
Assorted cotton fabrics

Oddments of embroidery canvas
Scissors
A black waterproof felt-tipped pen

Needlepoint and embroidery

Cat-herine's Collar

If you can't think what to give HER for Christmas, spend an evening using up old oddments of canvas and thread and make her an exclusive designer collar. This one is worked in half-cross stitch, using the pattern chart below. However, it would be a nice gesture if you came up with your own design, perhaps incorporating HER name in lurex threads, or stitching in some beads.

You will need:

A piece of 14 holes per inch (hpi), single-thread tapestry canvas measuring 14in x 2in (36cm x 5cm)

Oddments of Anchor stranded cotton (I used turquoise, yellow, fuschia, mauve, green, lime, yellow, red, orange, bright pink and black)
A ½in (1cm) buckle and loop
A piece of glove or chamois leather, 11½in x ½in (29cm x 1cm)
A tapestry (blunt-ended) needle
Masking tape
Copydex glue

To make the collar, first bind the edges of the canvas with masking tape to prevent it catching on the cottons. Then begin working from the chart in half-cross stitch, using four strands of cotton. Every symbol on the chart represents one stitch and the key indicates which symbol relates to which colour.

When the needlework is completed, remove the masking tape and turn the waste edges of canvas into the centre (trim if necessary). Glue these to the back of your work with Copydex. Trim and fold back the curved end and glue into position.

Place the buckle into position through the straight end, fold back the waste canvas and stitch down firmly. Thread the collar

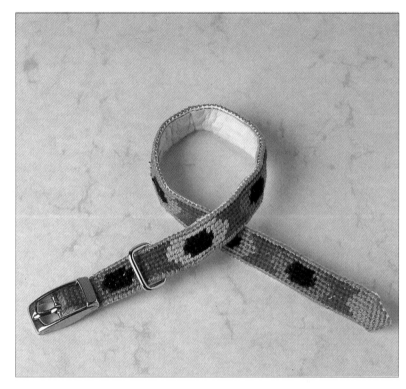

through the metal loop and slide it up to the buckle end, positioning it approximately 1½in (4cm) from the buckle. Catch into position with a stitch. Cut a strip of chamois leather to fit the complete length of the collar and glue into place. Make a series of holes with a needle through all thicknesses of fabric, discussing comfortable positions with your cat before proceeding.

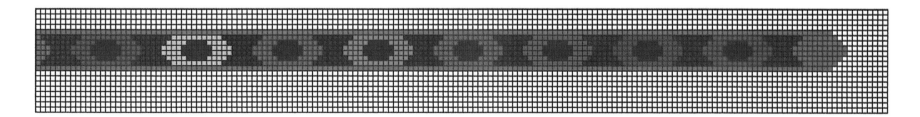

Cat Fob

Keep your keys safe on this cat fob and use up your scraps.

You will need:

2 pieces of 14 holes per inch (hpi) canvas, each 4in (10cm) square
Anchor stranded cottons in black, orange, beige and green
A key ring attachment (see Stockist Information, p.89)
A small amount of polyester wadding
A tapestry needle
Masking tape

To make the key fob, first bind your pieces of canvas with masking tape to prevent it catching on threads. Begin stitching, working in half-cross stitch and reading the chart below. Use four strands of cotton. When stitching is completed, trim and turn under raw edges of canvas and place back and front wrong sides together. Sew carefully together around the outside edge, leaving a gap for stuffing. Stuff and sew up gap. Sew key ring attachment to centre top.

The Cat's Whiskers

This baby bib would make a lovely gift from a young child to his/her new brother/sister. The design is stitched onto a very cheap bib (you can buy them in packs of three from baby shops such as Mothercare) and makes it look very special.

You will need:

A cheap white bib
Anchor stranded cotton in red, orange, blue and pink
An embroidery needle
An indelible pen or embroidery transfer pen

First trace off the template on p.85 and transfer it onto the centre of the bib. Using six strands of stranded cotton, stitch over the outline of the cat in backstitch, working the feet, arms and head in orange, the dungarees in red, the collar, tie and eyes in blue and the nose and mouth in pink.

Patchwork

The next three projects are made using patchwork or applique technique. Once you have made the needle case or the pin cushion you will want to go on to bigger and better things. All three were designed by Janet and Roger Quilter.

Patch the Pin Cushion

You will need:

Small pieces of cotton or polyester, 4in (10cm) square, in black, white and green

Red fabric for the background, 5in x 4in (12½cm x 10cm)
Patterned fabric for the back, 5in x 4in (12½cm x 10cm)
Polyester filling
A ruler
A marking pencil
A knitting needle or pencil

To make Patch, trace off all shapes from the template on p.81 onto the correct colours of fabric and cut out. Mark up the fabric and clip all curves.

Tack-hem curved sides of eyes (A). Position on upper part of head (B) and hem stitch into place. Tack-hem straight edge of cheeks (C)

(Continued overleaf)

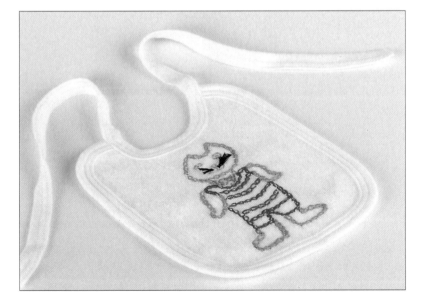

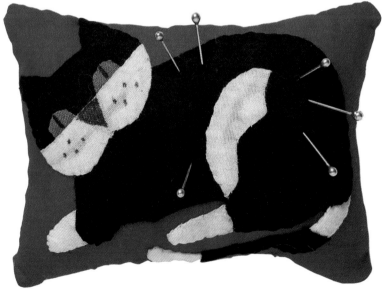

Patch the Pin Cushion (contd.)

and stitch to (B). Now tack round whole head shape. Tack round two sides of ears (D) to form rounded point. Stitch to top of head.

With waterproof felt-tipped pen, draw in pupil of eyes, upturned triangle for nose and spots on cheeks for whiskers (try pen on spare piece of fabric first to avoid 'blotting').

Tack-hem body (E). Add front paw (F), stitching in place. Tack-hem inner wavy line of white patch (G) and stitch to rear leg (H). Cut away excess black behind white patch. Add white paw (I) in similar fashion. Tack round whole back leg, position on body and stitch in place, changing thread to match. First stitch together the three pieces of tail (J, K and L) then hem round complete tail and stitch into place.

Press carefully but do not press seams open. Tack to background and stitch into place. Pin the background and back material together, right sides facing each other, with a ½in (1cm) seam allowance. Leave at the base an opening of about 2in (5cm). Machine or backstitch round cushion, strengthening stitching each side of opening. Turn to right side. Press well. Stuff firmly, pushing stuffing into the corners with a knitting needle or pencil. When firm, slip-stitch open seams together, if necessary pushing in a little more stuffing as you go.

Lavender may be used as an alternative stuffing.

Smokey the Needle Cat

You will need:

Small pieces of cotton or polycotton fabric in: A) mid grey B) light grey C) black D) dark crimson E) dark pink F) yellow

Background fabric for cover (here yellow), one piece 9in x 4in (23cm x 10cm)

Print fabric for lining, 9in x 4in (23cm x 10cm)

2 pieces of felt for book leaves, each 8in x 3in (20cm x 7cm)

Wadding (optional)

A piece of stiff white card, 8in x 3in (20cm x 7cm)

A fabric marking pencil

A craft knife

Masking tape

Pinking shears

N.B. When tracing shapes allow ¼in (½cm) extra for turnings. Clip all curves. Use blind-hem stitch throughout.

From the template on p.82, trace and cut out light grey cheeks (B), yellow eyes (F), black nose (C) and dark crimson mouth (D). Tack-hem all round cheeks. For eyes, nose and mouth, leave untacked the parts that are hidden under the cheeks. Stitch cheeks to mouth, taking care that cheeks just butt together. Trim away excess mouth fabric. Add nose and then eyes in similar fashion. With light grey (B) add lower lip.

Cut out head shape in (A) and tack-hem. Carefully position cheeks etc. and sew into place using appropriate coloured threads. With mid grey (A) and dark pink (E) cut out ears. Join the two colours at centre seam, then tack round whole shape. Stitch to head. With black pen, draw in eyes and dots on cheeks for whiskers. (try drawing with the pen on a scrap of fabric first to check that it does not run).

Press the head. With fabric marking pencil draw out a rectangle 8in x 3in (20cm x 7cm) on cover fabric. If you wish to pad the head, tack it to a piece of wadding then trim the wadding to the exact shape of the head. Position head on right side of cover and stitch in place.

With a craft knife, score a line at the centre of the cardboard to ease folding. Carefully line up with marked fabric. Fold over raw edges and trim to about ³⁄₄in (2cm). Temporarily 'anchor' in place with small pieces of masking tape. With double thread, stitch across from one long side to the other, pulling fabric tightly over card. It is advisable to start at the centre and work outwards. Finish off securely. Take care not to distort the head. Fold corners in on short sides and stitch in place. Press in raw edges of lining so that it is about ¹⁄₄in (¹⁄₂cm) smaller than cover. Hem into place. Cut felt 'pages' with pinking shears. Stitch to centre of cover with thread of matching colour.

Blodwen the Cat-er-pillow

There are two approaches you can take to this cushion. By now you should really be getting into patchwork, in which case you will want to make up the coverlet that Blodwen is sitting on using patches of fabric as indicated on the template on p.83. Alternatively, you can make the whole coverlet area using one piece of patterned fabric cut to the whole shape. Blodwen would prefer a patchwork quilt to sit on but don't let her head-rubbing influence your decision.

Basic equipment

Marking pencil
Glass-headed pins
Ruler
45° set square
Black waterproof felt pen
Drawing paper
A soft composite board that will take dressmaking pins
Small, sharp scissors

Patchwork fabric

Cotton or polycotton in the following colours and measurements:
A) black, 10in x 8in (25cm x 20cm)
B) white, 10in x 8in (25cm x 20cm)
C) orange, 10in x 8in (25cm x 20cm)
D) blue and white, 12in x 9in (30cm x 23cm)

(Continued on p.41)

Blodwen the Cat-er-pillow (contd.)

Small pieces of:
  E) *dark grey*
  F) *pale grey*
  G) *pink*
  H) *pale green*
For the coverlet, either a selection of
  scraps to make the 'patchwork
  quilt' effect or patterned fabric mea-
  suring 12in x 8in (30cm x 20cm)

Cushion cover

1 yard (1 metre) of 36in (91cm)-wide
  cotton or polycotton
16in (40cm) zip to match
18in (46cm) cushion pad
2oz (50g) wadding approximately 14in
  (35½cm) square

The picture is handsewn; the zip and final seaming can be machine sewn. Finished cushion measures 18in (46cm) square.

Preparation

Wash and press all fabrics. Make a swatch strip with code letters marked for quick and easy reference.

On the paper, draw an 11in (28cm) square and mark in lines 1in (2½cm) apart each way to form a grid. Transfer the design on p.83 square by square, each square representing 1in (2½cm). When complete, draw in the outline in black felt pen. Fill in fabric colour code for guidance. Add arrows on quilt.

Tips

Use the same colour thread as 'top' fabric or nearest darker shade when hemming into place. A blind-hem stitch is used throughout. Keep marking pencil well sharpened. It is advisable to cut out pieces as required as this is less confusing than cutting out all pieces at once. Try to keep fabric of basic picture with the grain horizontal (except when making up the coverlet – see quilt instructions).

Clip all curves. Cut away carefully any unnecessary bulk at the back of work, particularly where a darker fabric is behind a lighter one. Use the soft board as a working base. Pin drawing to board and leave in place for constant reference, pinning pieces into position before sewing together.

To make up quilt

The coverlet the cat is sitting on can be plain or patterned material or, as in the original design, made up of fabric scraps to represent a patchwork quilt. About ten different patterns have been used.

Cut several strips 8in long by 1in wide (20cm x 2½cm), marking a ¼in (½cm) seam line on both long sides on right side of fabric. Fold over one side and press. Pin to the next strip, lining up with unpressed seam line. Blind-hem together. Repeat in the desired sequence to make a complete piece approximately 12in x 8in (30cm x 20cm).

Cut out into the shapes indicated for the quilt, following the arrows for the directions of the strips. Sew together and add the wallpaper background. It is advisable to allow at least 1in (2½cm) round outside edge of quilt and wallpaper for later adjustment.

To make up cat

Cut out and tack-hem the coloured patches, leaving raw the edges which come at the edges of the body. Cut out the white main part of the body as a complete shape, applique patches, then trim away surplus white. Now tack-hem round whole body shape. This gives a cleaner line. Apply the same principle to the head, back legs and tail. Insert dark grey for the underbelly.

Trace and cut out black head and trim away dotted section. Cut out and tack-hem two white cheeks, two pale green eyes, a pale grey chin and a pink nose. Tack cheeks to chin, making sure that they just butt together above the chin. Trim away excess chin fabric, attach nose and eyes in similar fashion. Now hem stitch together. Sew ginger patch to top of head, tack-hem round whole head, sew cheeks etc. in place. Cut out ears in pink and black fabric and join centre seams, then tack-hem round complete ear. Stitch to head. With waterproof felt pen, carefully draw in pupil of eye and, if desired, a few spots on cheeks for whiskers.

Now make up tail and back legs, adding claws with felt pen. Stitch all pieces into place. Press cat and background, preferably with a steam iron. DO NOT press seams open. Stitch cat in position and carefully clip away excess fabric from background. Press again. Pin picture to the wadding so that it lies flat with no wrinkles. This is best done by pinning two opposite sides, then the other two and, finally, the four corners.

To make up cushion

For 11in (28cm) picture, cut out the following from the cushion cover fabric:

2 pieces 12in x 4½in (30½ x 11cm)
2 pieces 19in x 4½in (49 x 11cm)
2 pieces 19in x 10in (49cm x 25cm)

Turn under ½in (1cm) on one long side of each of the larger pieces and insert the zip about midway. Stitch together the seam above and below the zip. Take the four strips, turn under and tack ½in (1cm) hem on one side of each piece. Take a long strip, pin to short edge of smaller piece forming a right angle (check with set square). Tack in place. Repeat at other end of long strip, measuring to make sure that the inner sides of the two short strips are exactly 11in (28cm) apart. Add the fourth strip. You should have a completed surround with 11in (28cm) square opening. Hem together.

(Continued overleaf)

Knitting

Place over picture, centre up with surround, tack carefully into
   place, then hem, catching the wadding as you sew. If necessary, trim wadding at back to about ½in (1cm) from stitching. With wrong sides together, machine back of cushion to front with zip opening at the top. Turn and press seams. Do not press wadding. Insert cushion pad.

Paws to Knit

If you can knit one purl one you will be able to manage these simple, fun mittens knitted in double-knitting wool.

You will need:

*75g (3oz) double-knitting wool in a
   colour of your choice
A scrap of black wool for embroidery
A pair of 4.5mm needles
A blunt sewing needle*

Work to a tension of 16 stitches and 20 rows to 4in (10cm) square.
   Cast on 20 sts, work in stocking stitch (one row knit, next row purl) for 16in (41cm). Cast off. Fold in half and stitch up one side. On the other side, sew 3in (7cm), leave 3in (7cm) for the thumb opening, and sew to top.
   To knit the thumb, cast on 11 sts,* work in stocking stitch for 4 rows, decrease 1 st each side, repeat from * once more then ** work 4 rows, increase 1 st each side, repeat from **. Work 4 rows. Cast off. Sew both side seams and stitch to the side opening of the mitten – one left, one right. Embroider on eyes, nose, mouth and whiskers in black chain stitch, leaving loose ends for whiskers. Make a 20in (51cm) twisted cord from four lengths of wool and knot the ends. Thread this cord 1in (2½ cm) from the bottom edge of the mitten. Repeat for second mitten.

Wooden Cats

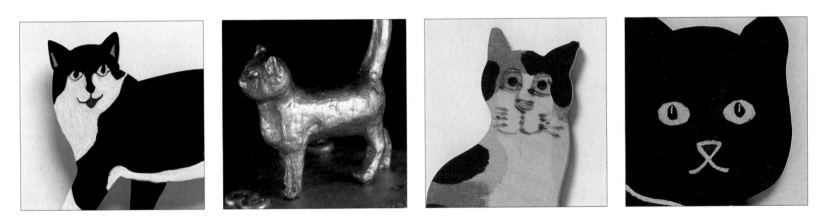

Basic Equipment

Offcuts of plywood, hardboard or
 MDF (medium density fibre
 board) or heavyweight
 cardboard
An electric jigsaw or fretsaw or a
 hand-held fretsaw

A clamp
Wood glue
Sandpaper
Water-based paints
Paintbrushes

I was brought up to believe that saws, electric drills and the like were strictly for the boys, which is why most of my work centres around fabrics, yarns and soft substances that can be modelled by hand. It was not until I inherited a somewhat ancient electric jigsaw that I realized a) how simple it was to use and b) that I could make all sorts of interesting things that I had previously considered beyond me.

The following projects can be made using either an electric jigsaw or a manual or electric fretsaw. Alternatively, they can be cut out of heavy cardboard with a craft knife or scissors.

Coat Cat-cher

I bought this basic wooden hook board from a market for next to nothing and decided it needed a cat. You can make the board from an odd piece of wood and cut the cat either from MDF, as I have, or from plywood, hardboard or card.

In addition to the basic equipment you will need:

For the hook board

A piece of wood approximately 9½in x 2½in (24cm x 7cm) and ½in (1cm) thick
2 1in (2½cm) brass screws
5 brass hooks
A hand or electric drill

For the cat

A piece of MDF board, 12in x 9in (30cm x 22½cm)
A black marker pen
White emulsion
A fine black felt-tipped pen
Water-based paints in black, white, pink and yellow
Polyurethane varnish
A pencil

To make the board, cut the wood to size and sand the edges. Drill two holes for screws approximately 1in (2½cm) in from each end, centring them carefully. Screw in hooks at equal intervals in between.

To make the cat, mark off every 1in (2cm) around all four edges of the MDF board with black marker pen, then join up these points to form a grid 12 squares tall by 9 squares wide. Turn to the template on p.76 and copy the cat shape onto your grid, square by square, being sure to draw the 'Coat-Cat-cher' tail. Clamp the wood to a table and saw carefully around the outline. Paint over the cutout with white emulsion and leave to dry. Draw on the facial features with a fine felt-tipped pen and also draw in markings of your choice. Paint in the markings in the appropriate colours and leave to dry. Add a second coat, dry and then add a coat of varnish.

Position the cat on the hook board, drawing in the position with a pencil. Spread wood glue liberally on the back of the cat's paws and press down onto board (support the weight of the top of the cat with a book or other object the same height as the board). Leave to dry thoroughly.

Cat-rina's Treasure Box

Any self-respecting cat needs somewhere to put her spare collar, her toy mouse and her flea comb. This box is made from simple cutouts of plywood glued together. The scrolls are made with FIMO and the cat itself can be modelled from either FIMO or papier mâché.

In addition to the basic equipment you will need:

2 pieces of 5mm plywood
*   measuring 4¼in (10½cm) square*
4 pieces of 5mm plywood
*   measuring 3¾in (9½cm) square*
1 piece of 5mm plywood
*   measuring 3½in (9cm) square*
A block of white FIMO
Gold enamel paint

To make the box, first cut the plywood (or you can use cardboard) to size. Take the four pieces measuring 3¾in (9½cm) square and glue them together, inside edge to outside edge, to form a perfect cube (see diagram, p.81). When the cube is dry, place it dead centre on one of the two pieces of plywood measuring 4¼in (10½cm) square and glue it down so that this forms a base. Take the two remaining pieces of plywood, centre the smaller square on the bigger one and glue them together to form the lid.

To make the scrolls, roll out sausages of FIMO and curl them into scroll shapes. Bake them in the oven following manufacturer's instructions. Model the cat from FIMO or papier mâché (see these chapters, pp.8–24), making the cat 2½in (6cm) in length. When the FIMO scrolls are cooked hard, glue them into position on the box sides and top and paint all pieces with two coats of gold paint. Paint the cat and then glue him to the top of the box to form a handle.

Frosty Cats

I found these wonderful fridge magnets on sale at Camden Lock Market in London, where they are designed and produced by Bob Mitchell. A small selection has been reproduced here with his kind permission. If, however, you are in London during a weekend, do go and see his whole range which includes mirrors as well as hundreds of different cat magnets, all extremely reasonably priced (see Stockist Information, p.89). This book provides templates for the shapes alone, as I expect you will want to paint on your favourite colourings and expressions. Please also note that Bob's designs are his copyright and may not be made for re-sale.

In addition to the basic equipment you will need:

Plywood, hardboard or cardboard
*Magnets**
White emulsion
Water-based paints in colours of your
  choice
A pencil
A fine drawing pen

*Magnetic self-adhesive tape can be bought by the yard and you just snip off as much as you need. Alternatively, you can buy craft magnets in various sizes. See Stockist Information, p.89.

To make these cats, trace off the templates on p.76 onto the plywood. Clamp the wood to a table and carefully cut around the shapes with an electric jigsaw or a fretsaw. Smooth the edges with sandpaper and coat the shape with white emulsion. When dry, draw on the basic markings with a pencil and then go over the facial features with a fine drawing pen. Paint in the markings colour by colour, leaving one to dry before applying a second. Glue the magnet onto the back.

N.B. You can also make cat magnets from FIMO or papier mâché.

Board Cat

Hang this cat in the kitchen and chalk on items such as sardines, pilchards, catnip, pickled mice, flea powder etc., as you run out of them.

In addition to the basic equipment you will need:

1 piece of plywood or hardboard measuring 14in x 11in (35cm x 27½cm)
A small tin of blackboard paint
A piece of orange felt, 6in (15cm) square
A scrap of polyester wadding (cotton wool would do)
A black felt-tipped pen
A scrap of Velcro or self-sealing tape
Chalk
White and yellow water-based paints
String
A self-adhesive picture hook
Copydex glue
Scissors

To make this cat, first take the plywood and mark off every 1in (2½ cm) along all four sides with a black marker pen. Join up these points to form a grid 14 squares wide by 11 squares tall. Turn to the template on p.84 and copy the cat shape square by square onto your grid. Clamp the wood to a table and carefully saw out the shape using an electric jigsaw or a fretsaw. Smooth the edges with sandpaper. Paint the whole shape with three coats of blackboard paint, leaving each one to dry before adding the next.

While the paint is drying, trace off the fish shape onto the orange felt, fold the felt in half and cut through both thicknesses. Cut a circle of polyester wadding slightly smaller than the body of the fish. Draw an eye onto one fish shape with a black felt-tipped pen. Glue the front and back pieces of the fish together around the edges, sandwiching the wadding in between. Stick a small piece of Velcro or self-sealing tape onto the back of the fish, gluing the other half onto the board.

With chalk, roughly draw in the eyes, nose, mouth, cheek and tail outline onto the board. Carefully paint over these using yellow for the eyes and white for the other details. Wrap a length of string repeatedly around the chalk and tie it securely, then glue the other end to the back of the cat board. Stick a self-adhesive picture hook onto the top centre back of the board.

Catmobile

This is a fun project for a child to make and I can prove it because this one was made by my child, Justine, aged 22½ (years, that is). The cats are made from cardboard, with felt glued on. If you don't have any felt, use fancy wrapping paper or photograph your cat in various positions and make a mobile from photographic cutouts.

In addition to the basic equipment you will need:

12in (30cm) squares of felt in orange, white and black
1 yard (1 metre) of ½in (1cm) black ribbon or tape
2 sticks, each approximately 12in (30cm) long
A ¾in (2cm) panel pin
6 small screw-in eyes for hanging
Black cotton
A sheet of A4 medium-weight cardboard
Scissors
Copydex glue
A black marker pen
White paint or liquid typewriter correction fluid

To make the Catmobile, first trace off the templates on p.86 onto cardboard and cut out the shapes. Then trace them onto the coloured felt, making two images (one in reverse) for each shape. Glue these onto the front and back of the cutouts. Cut feature details out of contrasting felt and glue these into position.

Add fine details, either in black pen or in white paint or correction fluid, depending on the colour of the felt background. Cut 1½in (4cm) lengths of ribbon or tape and glue these onto the centre top of each figure.

Take the two sticks and join them together at the centre with the panel pin. Screw in eyes at each end of both sticks and top and bottom of the centre point where they cross. Tie lengths of cotton to the screw-in eyes and attach figures by tying the loose ends of cotton to the ribbon loops. Finally, tie a piece of cotton to the centre top, screw in eye and attach mobile to the ceiling.

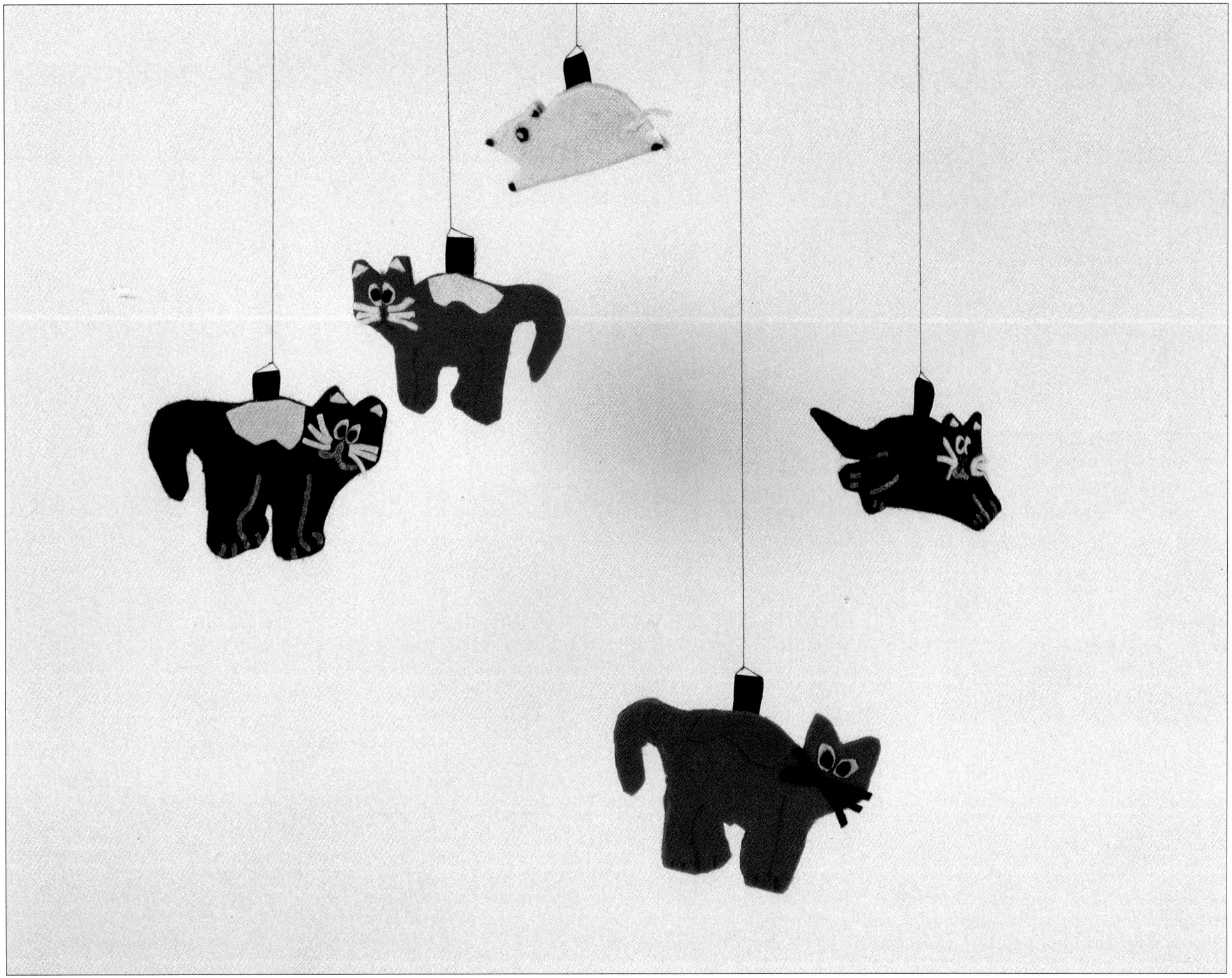

Painted Cats

Your cat's portrait can and should be painted anywhere and everywhere. Your only limitation is the type of paints you use, as you should bear in mind the material you are working on and whether your masterpiece is going to be hung, worn, drunk from or displayed indoors or outdoors.

There is a vast number of specialist paints available for working on everything from fabric to glass (see Stockist Information, p.89). Don't feel limited by the items I have chosen to paint – use the ideas and adapt them to decorate anything you feel like.

Basic Equipment

Painting on metal, enamel and wood

Paints (see specific project instructions)
Artist's and household brushes
Polyurethane gloss varnish
Nail or scrubbing brushes
Liquid detergent
Paint and rust remover
Rubber gloves and a face mask
Sandpaper (medium and fine)
Wire wool
Plastic filler
Wood sealer
Cotton rags and white spirit

Painting on silk

Silk paints (I recommend Marabu and Deka products)
Artist's paintbrushes
Gutta pens in various colours
An iron and ironing board
A piece of muslin or cloth

Painting on glass

Glass stain
A tube of liquid lead (see Stockist Information, p.89)
An eye dropper

Painting on metal, enamel and wood

The technique for these projects has been taken from the traditional art of barge or narrow boat painting. The items were designed and painted by Penny Newman who has, by special request, incorporated felines into her normally traditional designs. She has painted on various old items that can be picked up at junk and car boot sales but you must be sure to follow the instructions for preparation in order to get the best results.

Preparation of old metal, enamel and wooden items

First place the article in hot water and scrub it thoroughly with washing-up liquid and a hard brush. Rinse and dry. If the article has old paint on it strip this off with paint stripper, taking care to wear rubber gloves and a mask. If that won't remove it use sandpaper. If the article is rusty, remove rust with a steel wool or rust proofer following manufacturer's instructions. If the item has any holes in it these can be filled with plastic filler and then sanded down to a smooth finish.

If you are working with a good-quality enamel hobby paint such as Humbrol Colour, you can paint the background coat directly onto your metal item. If, however, your item is made of wood, you should treat it with two coats of wood sealer before painting on it. There is also no need to strip the old paint from wooden items provided it can be sanded down to a smooth finish. Always remember to clean your paintbrushes after use with an old rag dipped in white spirit.

Bis-cat Tin

You will need:

A suitable tin with a lid
Humbrol Colour paints in crimson,
 yellow and midnight blue
½in (1cm) household paintbrush
Medium and fine artist's brushes
Masking tape
A wax crayon

Prepare the tin according to the instructions above. To paint it, first wrap a piece of masking tape around the bottom and top of the base and, with a household paintbrush, paint the area in between in two coats of red. (Always leave the first coat to dry before applying the second.)

While that is drying, divide the lid into nine segments by ruling across the middle with your wax

(Continued overleaf)

Bis-cat Tin (contd.)

crayon. Carefully paint two coats of red paint on every third segment using a medium artist's brush. When the base is dry, peel off the masking tape and fill in the blank areas with blue. Paint in three blue segments on the lid. Leave to dry, then with your wax crayon mark positions for evenly-spaced yellow dots along the blue base and evenly-spaced cats around the tin itself. Paint in the cats in yellow with a fine artist's brush using the template on p.82 as a guide. Paint in the yellow triangles on the lid. Add the umbrellas. Leave to dry and add two coats of varnish.

Cats in the Moonlight

This design is painted on an old enamel dish prepared according to the instructions on p.51. The outline for the cat is on p.82. Use Humbrol Colour paints.

To paint this dish, start with the blue background and when completely dry add the border in red. Paint in the brown tree trunk using a medium artist's brush, and use a fine brush to create the branches and twigs. Add the green leaves with a medium brush and then add the pears. When completely dry, paint in the white cats and the moon, then add two coats of varnish.

Fat Cat

This is my cat Sparky, who can usually eat a horse. It's a nice, simple painting job and the template appears on p.88.

As well as the basic equipment, you will need:

An enamel bowl
Enamel paints in yellow and black (I have used Deka-Lac water-based enamels)
A chinagraph pencil

First paint the inside of the bowl with three coats of yellow paint, taking care to let each coat dry before applying the next. Then turn to the template on p.88 and, working by eye with a chinagraph pencil, draw in the outline for the cat and dividing lines for the markings. Fill in the appropriate areas with black paint using a medium-sized artist's brush, leave to dry and add an extra coat of black. Leave to dry and then paint on two coats of varnish.

Cuppy-Cat

Penny has painted her design on an ordinary white china cup and saucer using Humbrol paints. However, if you want to use a cup I suggest you buy special ceramic paints that can be fixed to the china in the oven. Follow the basic instructions for the biscuit tin on p.51, using the template on p.82 for the cats. This design uses the smaller version, with three cats placed at equal distances around the cup.

Cat Tra-il

Jolly up an old wooden tray with these prancing Chinchillas (opposite). First prime the tray with wood sealer and then paint it on both sides with two coats of blue. When dry, paint in the rim in red. Paint the tree trunks in brown, leaving equal distances between and at each side of them. The tree-tops are painted with random swirly lines of green and then the apples are added in red and the leaves (one dab of a medium-sized artist's brush) in a lighter green. Draw in the cats from the larger template on p.82 and paint in white. Paint in some simple flowers along the bottom of the design. Add the cats' facial features and paws with a very fine artist's brush. Varnish.

Painting on silk

Silk painting is great fun and the range of equipment on the market makes it very simple to learn the technique. The best paints in my opinion sell under the trade names Marabu and Deka (see Stockist Information, p.89). I have used a mixture of both for these projects. Both of these ranges are water soluble so you can lighten a colour by adding water and mix colours as you please.

They can be fixed by ironing the silk at a cotton temperature after you have finished your design. The colours will not fix until they are ironed, so if you make a mistake with your painting you can just wash it out. Always wash and iron silk before beginning your painting to remove any sizing.

The basic technique used for most of the following designs involves drawing in an outline with 'gutta'. You can buy gutta outliner pens in several colours as well as transparent and their job is to stop the colours running into each other. Another technique that can produce interesting results is the watercolour technique. You paint the colours directly onto the silk and let them run into each other. You can add detail in black when they are dry or draw it in before beginning with a coloured gutta pen.

You can buy silk by the yard or metre in various thicknesses and you can also buy made-up items like the tie, ready to paint on (see Stockist Information, p.89).

Hand-cat-chief

This design (see overleaf) is taken from the template used for 'Blodwen the Cat-er-pillow' on p.83. To make this bit of finery you will need:

A piece of white silk, 18½in (47cm)
  square
A clear and a bronze gutta pen
Silk paints in aqua, fuchsia, royal,
  yellow, black and orange
Fuchsia sewing cotton
A frame measuring 18in (45cm)
  square (see Fabricated Cats, p.27)
Masking tape
Drawing pins
A sheet of A3 paper
A thick black felt-tipped pen
Water
A fine sewing needle

First wash and iron the silk square. Then take your frame and cover the top edge with masking tape. Pin the silk square onto the frame, placing drawing pins approximately every 1in (2½cm), stretching it until it is taut. Take the sheet of A3 paper and draw with thick black felt-tipped pen a square 11in x 11in (27½cm x 27½cm). Mark off every 1in (2½cm) along all four sides of the square and join up these points to form a grid of 1in (2½cm) squares. Turn to p.83 and copy the design onto your grid, square by square. Place the paper under the frame and you should be able to see the outline through the silk. If you can't, attach it to the back of the silk with masking tape.

Practise using the gutta pen on paper first to achieve the correct pressure to draw clear lines without blobs. When you can do this, draw in all outlines except the facial features in clear gutta using the tracing as a guide. Leave the gutta to dry for about half an hour and then draw in the facial features using a bronze gutta pen.

Starting with the background so you get a feel of how much paint you need, fill in the areas between the gutta outlines in the appropriate colours, using the photograph as a guide. The green is achieved by mixing blue and yellow, and I have watered this mixture down and added a drop of orange to make the beige. Finally add the border in fuchsia and leave the painting to dry for at least an hour.

Place it on an ironing board, right side down, and iron over a piece of muslin or cloth at cotton temperature. Carefully roll and stitch the edges to finish off the square.

Hand-cat-chief

Greeting Cats

Use up oddments of silk to make these greeting cards. All except the Calico long-haired cat are produced using the same technique as the 'Hand-cat-chief'.

Trace off your designs from printed greeting cards of cats or from photographs, magazines or book illustrations, then add your own colourings and surroundings.

The Calico cat was produced using the watercolour technique. First the facial features were drawn in with bronze gutta, then a border was painted across the top in blue. Pussy's coat is a mixture of black, white and a brown which I made by mixing green, red and white. The eyes are painted in in yellow. You can buy the mounts ready-made or cut them yourself from card (see Stockist Information, p.89)

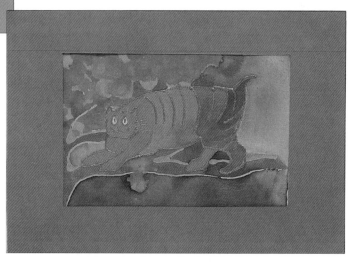

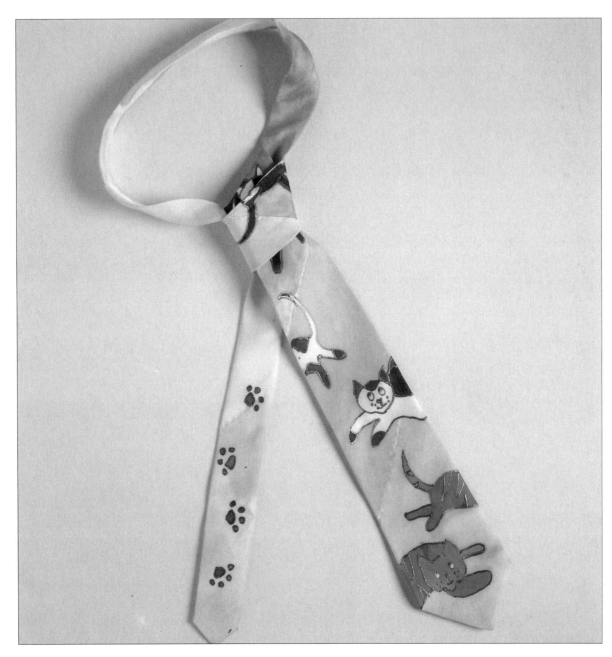

Tie and Tails

Only a real man would wear this tie, so be careful who you make it for.

You will need:

A white silk tie (see Stockist
   Information, p.89)
Bronze and transparent gutta
Silk paints in pink, yellow, aqua,
   black, orange and mauve
A hard pencil

To make this tie, first draw onto it your cats using a well-sharpened hard pencil that will give you a very fine line. Draw in head and paws at one side of the tie and rear legs and tails just above at the other side. Draw three cats in all, finishing at the point where you would make the tie knot. At the other end of the tie, draw in four paw pads. Cover the outlines with bronze gutta and leave to dry for about an hour. Fill in the cats with orange or black, leaving intended white areas plain. Fill in paw pads in black.

When they are dry, divide the tie into sections by drawing on diagonal lines in between each cat using transparent gutta. Leave the gutta for half an hour and paint in the different areas of background colour, watering the paints down so that you get a pastel effect. Leave to dry, then fix by ironing on the wrong side over a piece of muslin or cloth at cotton temperature.

Painting on glass

There is really no excuse for having any area in your home that does not feature a cat. Once you have painted your crockery, your walls and your furniture you can start on your windows, using a special glass paint. These little dangling circles are good practice for you and can be bought with the surround and chain already attached (see Stockist Information, p.89). They are available in several sizes. Alternatively you can get glass circles cut at your local glazier and buy the leaded edging on a roll to attach yourself.

Green Punk Cat God

To make this cat you will need:

A glass circle with chain, 4in (10cm) in diameter (see Stockist Information, p.89)
A tube of liquid lead (see Stockist Information, p.89)
Bottles of glass stain in green, yellow and blue
An eye dropper

The liquid lead is used to draw the black dividing lines that will make your painted glass look like real stained glass. It comes in a squeezy tube and the width of your line depends on the size of the hole you make in the top of the tube. Before applying the lead to your glass, bear in mind the following hints:

1. For uniform lines apply constant pressure on the tube.

2. Before beginning each new line, wipe the tip of the tube.

3. Hold the tube at a 45° angle to the glass.

4. Touch the tip to the glass and start squeezing.

5. Lift the bottle about 1½in (4cm) above the work surface and follow the lines of your pattern.

6. As you complete each line, touch the tip down to the glass, stop squeezing and pull the bottle away.

(Continued overleaf)

Green Punk Cat God (contd.)

7. If you make a mistake, wipe off instantly with a wet cloth or wait until the line is dry and scrape off with a craft knife.

To make the Punk Cat God, trace off the template on p.85 and place it in position under the glass circle. Using the application methods above, draw in the outlines with liquid lead and leave to set for half an hour. Fill an eye dropper with green stain and apply it a drop at a time between the outlines, letting it spread out until you achieve the required depth of colour. Leave to dry and then fill in the cat's earring with yellow stain. Fill in the outer circle in the same way using blue stain.

Cat at the Window

You will need:

A glass circle with chain, 4in (10cm) in diameter
A tube of liquid lead
Glass stain in green, blue, yellow and red
An eye dropper
A fine paintbrush

To make this cat, follow the instructions for the 'Green Punk Cat God' but use the template for the 'Cat at the Window' on p.85. After you have applied the liquid lead, flood-fill the cat's body, legs and head with yellow stain using an eye dropper. Flood-fill the window panes in blue using the eye dropper. Leave to dry and then carefully paint in the check green curtains and the cat's markings in red using a fine brush.

Print and Paper

There are all sorts of lovely things you can do with paper that will amuse your cats and keep the children busy at the same time. Decoupage is a great way to use all those pretty cat pictures you find in magazines, and, with simple printing techniques, you can make your own stationery and wrapping paper from plain boring old stuff. In this section I have also included a party mask which is made from cardboard covered in felt. I have done this because a) you could easily use a fancy paper instead of felt and b) I couldn't find another suitable cat-egory to include it in.

Decoupage

'Decoupage', or the art of cutting and sticking, was popular during the late seventeenth and eighteenth century and was designed to imitate the freehand painting incorporated in highly-prized 'lacquerware' which was imported into Europe from the Far East.

Many specialist papers were produced for this simple scissor art with beautiful cutouts that you glue to an item requiring decoration, then hand colour and coat with numerous layers of varnish. The overall effect of the project will depend entirely on your selection and arrangement of cutouts, but here are a couple of simple ideas to start you off.

Street Cats

This is a box to keep your useful thingummyjigs in.

In addition to the basic equipment you will need:

A wooden cigar box
2 squares of fabric with which to line it
1 yard (1 metre) of braid
Paper cutouts of cats
Cutouts of houses
2 paper fasteners (the type with two
*   prongs that bend back)*
12in (30cm) of narrow ribbon

To make this box, first cut out your fabric to fit the inside of the box lid and the inside base of the box. Stick it into position with Copydex, smoothing out any creases or bubbles. Glue braid around the edges to create a neat finish.

Next, cut out a collection of houses and rooftops and arrange them on the lid of the box. Glue them down with a paper glue stick. Cut out the cats, arrange them above and between the houses and glue into position. Cover the edges of the box with a paper that matches the colourway and then stick a row of cats on the top.

Paint at least three coats of varnish over your composition, leaving each coat to dry before adding the next. Make a hole through the centre front of the lid and push through a paper fastener, folding back the prongs underneath. Do the same at the centre front of the box and secure with narrow ribbon.

If you prefer, use cutouts of flowers instead of houses, to create a garden scene.

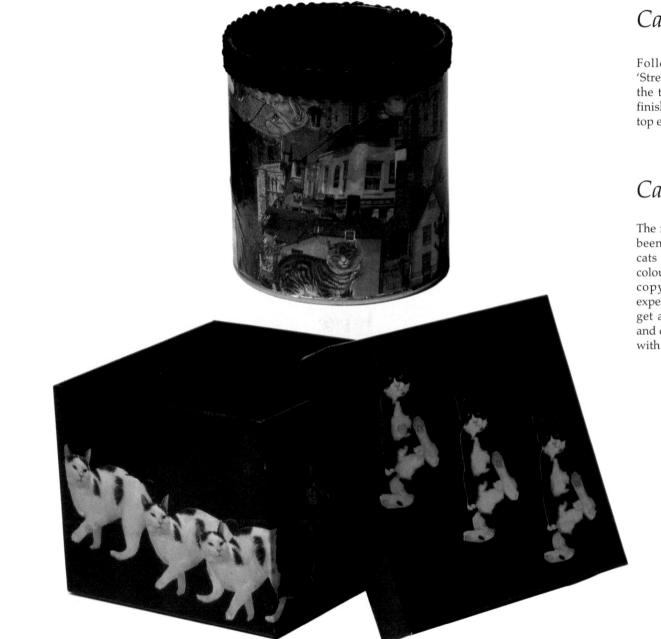

Cat Tin

Follow the instructions for the 'Street Cats' box on p.62, but line the tin with wrapping paper and finish by gluing braid around the top edge.

Cat Box

The repeat motifs on this box have been produced by gluing all the cats onto one sheet and getting a colour copy from the local photo-copy shop. This can be quite expensive and you might prefer to get a black and white photocopy and colour the cats in yourself with with felt-tipped pens.

Pencil Drum

You can make lovely black and white arrangements using photocopies, which are especially appropriate if you happen to have a black and white cat. This pencil drum is made from an old cocoa tin covered in plain coloured paper. For the basic decoupage technique, see instructions for 'Street Cats' on p.62.

Printing

You can print using potatoes, pencil erasers or lino if you are feeling really clever. You can also cut stencils from card to decorate no end of things. You can use printing inks or acrylic paints to achieve interesting effects. Print onto plain paper or wrapping paper or cut up the back of old greeting cards to make gift tags.

Cat Wrap

This simple design is made by potato printing. Wrap up your cat in his own printed paper and post him off to your grandma for Christmas.

In addition to the basic equipment you will need:

A sheet of plain paper or brown wrapping paper
A large potato
A piece of card
A felt-tipped pen
A knitting needle

To make the wrapping paper, turn to the templates for either the mobile on p.86 or the fridge magnets on p.76 and trace off your favourite shape onto cardboard. Cut it out, cut the potato in half and place the card template on it. Trace around the outside with a felt-tipped pen then cut away all the potato that is not inside your outline. Make two holes for eyes with a knitting needle, cover the finished cat in paint or ink and stamp it onto the paper.

A Letter from your Cat

Send an important missive from pussy on his own notepaper. You can also use your stamp as a seal on the envelope and once you have cut the design it is there for you to use again and again.

In addition to the basic equipment you will need:

Plain notepaper
A pencil eraser
Acrylic paint or an ink-pad

The design for the notepaper has been cut from a pencil eraser. Trace off the template on p.88 onto the eraser. With a craft knife, cut away all the areas you do not wish to print. Press onto an ink-pad or paint with acrylic paint and print.

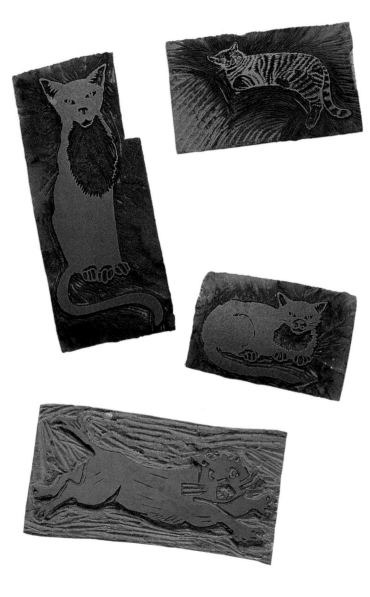

Lino Cat

Lino cutting is great fun but there are a couple of basic precautions you should take to prevent you gouging out sections of your hand instead of the lino. If you have a clamp, clamp the lino to a table to stop it slipping, or alternatively work up against a wall. Once you have made your lino cut it is a good idea to mount it (nail it) onto a block of wood to keep it flat. The prints on coloured paper are from a simple cut printed with acrylic paints (you will find the template on p.88). The black and white prints are produced with oil-based ink and you can trace the design directly from the prints as they appear here.

In addition to the basic equipment you will need:

A piece of lino 6in x 4in (15cm x 10cm)
Lino cutting tools
A roller
A sheet of glass, ceramic tile or piece of Formica
Oil-based printing ink
An old dessert spoon
White spirit
Old rags
Pieces of paper or card to be decorated

Trace off the template on p.88 or the black and white prints opposite onto the lino. Use the knife tool for outlining any smooth lines required: V tools for narrow lines and U tools for cutting large areas, clearing backgrounds etc. Remember that the areas you cut away will be white and those you leave will print. To check how your block is progressing, place a piece of thin scrap paper over the block and make a rubbing with a pencil.

When your cutting is complete, take the printing ink and squeeze a small amount (like toothpaste) onto the glass. Roll it with the roller until you have an even patch and the roller is covered (there should be a sound like Velcro ripping as you roll back and forth – not a squishy mess that will fill up the lines in the block).

Now ink up the block evenly by rolling the roller back and forth and from side to side. Get a clean piece of paper (it's best to have a pile cut to size, ready on the printing table), place over the block and hold firmly into position while rubbing gently but firmly with the flat of a spoon handle in circular motions all over the print. When you are satisfied that you have covered the whole area, carefully peel back the paper and leave somewhere to dry (away from the cat unless you want paw marks as well).

When you have finished, clean the block, roller and glass with white spirit.

Cat Mask

You too can go to the ball and you can hide behind this exquisitely feathered and bejewelled Cat Mask. If you don't want to go, send your favourite Persian who is certain to enjoy the occasion and already has a suitable fur coat to wear.

To make this Cat Mask you will need:

2 A4 pieces of card
A piece of felt or wrapping paper
    12in x 8in (30cm x 20cm)
4 gold pipe cleaners
2 black feathers
A 12in (30cm) stick
2 yards (2 metres) of gold sequins
1 yard (1 metre) each of mauve and
    silver sequins
3 green sequins
A craft knife
Copydex glue

To make the mask, first trace off the template on p.87 onto the two sheets of card and cut out, once with the nose shape (for the front of the mask) and once following the dotted line (for the back). Cut out the eyes from both pieces, then lay aside the back piece to use later. Cut out the shape (with a nose) from the felt or wrapping paper, adding ½in (1cm) all round. Glue this to the front of the mask, gluing the waste edges to the back. At the eye holes, clip around the waste and fold and glue to the back. Lay the stick onto the backing piece of the mask about 1in (2½ cm) away from the left eye hole with the end level with the top of the mask. Glue this down. Glue feathers to the top corners, then glue the front of the mask on top. Fold the four pipe cleaners in half and glue them at the fold onto the back of the nose, two each side to form eight whiskers.

Beginning about 1½in (4cm) from the bottom of the stick, wrap the gold string of sequins around the stick, gluing as you go. Do the same with the silver string and then add the mauve, winding it around the empty bottom area several times before spiralling it up the stick. Glue a border of gold sequins around the mask itself and dot sequins onto the mask front. Add a green sequin at each corner and one in the centre top.

Edible Cats

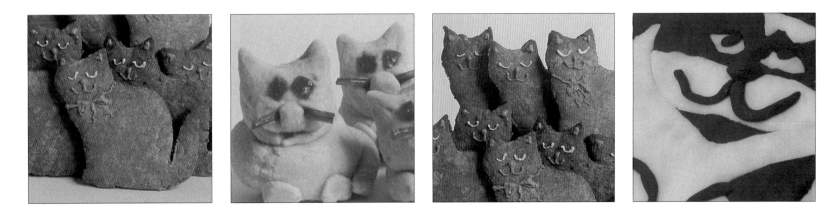

I planned in this section to give you recipes for kittens in custard, cat and mouse pie and *pommes des chats*. Unfortunately the ingredients are quite hard to come by, requiring an element of violence in their acquisition. For this reason I am just going to pass on a couple of old family favourites which I hope you will enjoy making and eating.

Ginger Cat Biscuits

You can buy biscuit cutters to make almost any shape from stars to dinosaurs, but for some reason I found it impossible to buy a cat shape. Through trial and error, however, I discovered that you can make a cardboard template of any of the smaller cats featured in the template section of this book (see pp.76–88) and simply place it on your biscuit dough and cut around it with a paring knife to make the shape. Judy Newman made the biscuits in these recipes and the cats and I ate the results.

To make these biscuits you will need:

8oz (200g) plain flour
1 level tsp bicarbonate of soda
3–4 level tsp ground ginger (depend-
* ing on your taste for it)*
2–3 level tsp cinnamon
4 level tsp caster sugar
4oz (100g) butter
6oz (150g) golden syrup
Icing or dried fruit to decorate

First trace off the image of your choice onto a sheet of clean white card. Cut out the shape with a craft knife to form a cardboard template. Sift together flour, bicarbonate of soda, ginger, cinnamon and sugar into a bowl. Melt butter and stir in syrup. Stir these into the dry ingredients and mix well until you have a stiff doughy mixture.

Roll out onto a floured board until the dough is about ⅛in (3mm) thick. Place the cardboard template lightly on the rolled-out dough and cut around the shape with a pointed knife. Place cut-out cats onto a greased baking tray. Bake at gas mark 5 (375°F/190°C) for 15–20 minutes. Place on a cooling rack until cold. Decorate with icing.

N.B. If you are no dab paw at icing, insert currants for the eyes, a piece of cherry for the mouth and angelica for whiskers before baking. Store in an airtight tin.

Marzicats

These delicious fat, sugary, everything-that's-bad-for-you cats melt in the mouth and are well worth dieting for a week for. I dare you.

You will need:

8oz (225g) icing sugar
8oz (225g) caster sugar
1lb (450g) ground almonds
1 tsp vanilla essence
2 eggs, lightly beaten
2 tsp lemon juice
Glacé cherries and angelica for
    decoration

Sift icing sugar into a bowl and mix with caster sugar and almonds. Add the essence with enough egg and lemon juice to mix to a stiff dough. Form into a ball and knead lightly.

To shape the cats, make one ball (or sausage, if you want the cat lying down) for the body and a smaller one for the head, pinching out the ear shapes. To make the face roll three pea-sized (petit pois) balls and squash two of them flat onto the face to form the cheeks. Place the third above centre for the nose. Roll a sausage shape and attach for the tail, moulding it around the body from centre back to centre front. Roll two more small balls for the feet. To make the eyes, push in small pieces of glacé cherry. Cut a piece of angelica into narrow strips and use them for the whiskers. Insert the knife under the cheeks and pull down slightly to form an open mouth.

Place the modelled cats onto a greased baking tray and bake in a very low oven ($\frac{1}{2}$ gas mark or 250°F / 120°C, for 4–5 hours or until they start to brown. Remove from oven and leave on baking tray until cold. Store in an airtight container.

Cat Cake

This is a recipe for non-cooks since I discovered that you can buy ready-to-roll fondant icing in a variety of colours and you can also buy ready-to-ice cakes from your local supermarket. I have included a recipe for fondant icing just in case you want to start from scratch. The cake you choose to cover is very much a matter of personal taste so I suggest you just use your favourite traditional fruit cake recipe.

You will need:

4½oz (125g) black fondant icing
4½oz (125g) white fondant icing
7oz (200g) red fondant icing
A round fruit cake, approximately 6in (15cm) in diameter
Apricot jam

To make fondant icing you will need:

1lb (450g) icing sugar
1 egg white
2oz (55g) liquid glucose (obtainable at chemists)
Vegetable colourings in black and red

Sift the icing sugar into a bowl and make a well in the centre. Add the egg white and the liquid glucose and beat these ingredients with a wooden spoon, scraping in all the icing sugar from the edges of the bowl. Divide into three portions and add appropriate vegetable colouring. Knead the mixture with your hands, adding a little icing sugar to prevent it sticking, and then wrap it in a polythene bag and store it in a cool place until you need it. Knead it again before use.

To ice the cake, photocopy and if necessary enlarge the template on p.88 and mark each section with a letter to represent a colour: 'A' for white, 'B' for black and 'C' for background, in this case red. Cut these paper colour sections out like a jigsaw. Rebuild the picture from these cutouts and lay it in front of you.

Coat the top of your cake with a thin layer of apricot jam to help the icing stick. Roll out the red icing and lay the templates marked 'C' on top of it. Cut out the shapes with a sharp knife and place them in position on top of the cake. Repeat this process for the black and white sections, rolling small pieces of black icing for the mouth. When you have completed the top of the cake, cut a strip of red icing and wrap this around the side (back) of the cake to correspond with the red background. Cut a strip of white icing and place this around the side (front). Smooth joins with your fingers and then eat great scrumptious chunks of your masterpiece.

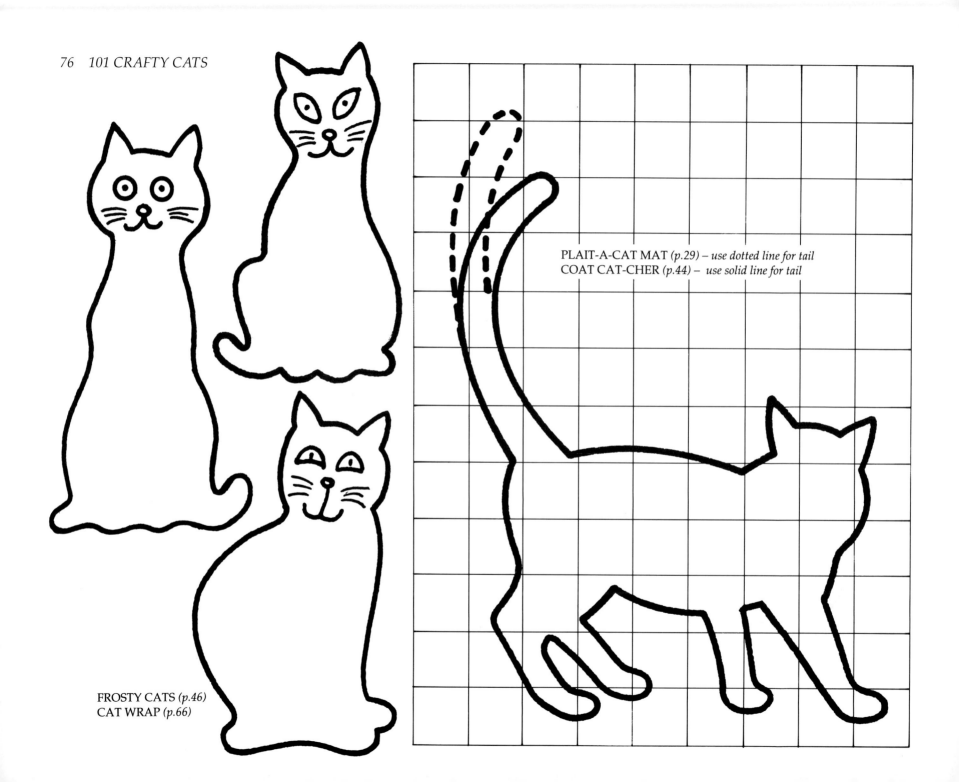

PLAIT-A-CAT MAT *(p.29)* – *use dotted line for tail*
COAT CAT-CHER *(p.44)* – *use solid line for tail*

FROSTY CATS *(p.46)*
CAT WRAP *(p.66)*

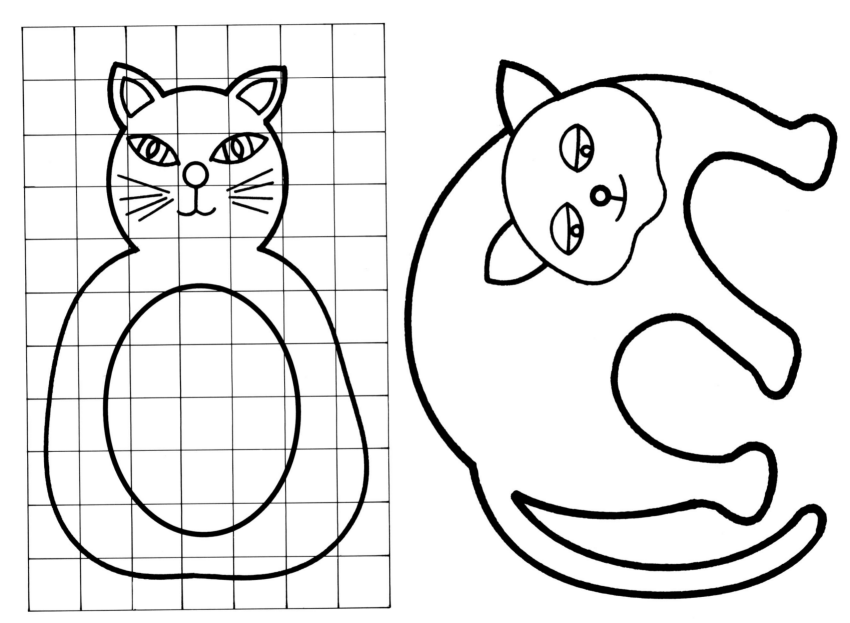

PURR-FECT IMAGE *(p.11)*   DISHY CAT *(p.16)*

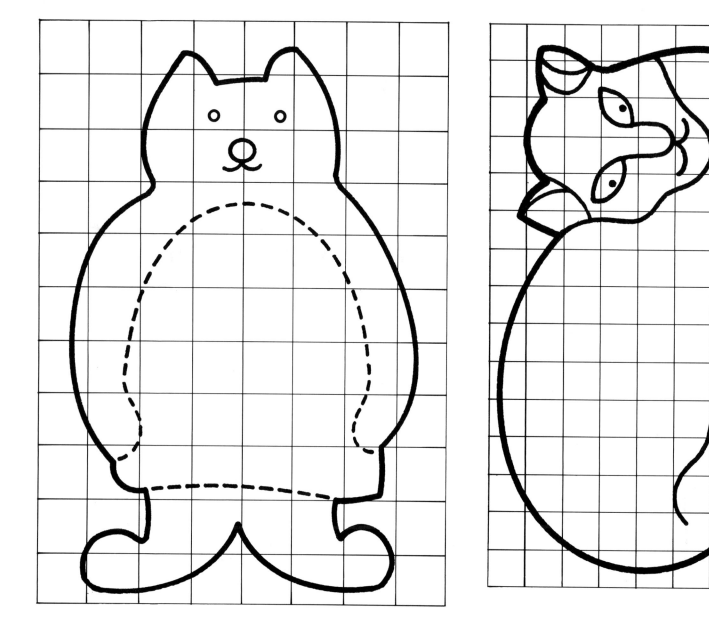

CAT A LIST *(p.18)*   HOOKED-ON CAT *(p.26)*

A = TAN
B = PURPLE
C = BLUE
D = MAUVE
E = CREAM
F = WHITE
G = EMERALD
H = DARK GREEN
I = YELLOW
J = PEACH
K = RED

OUTLINES = BLACK

BAG A CAT *(p.27)*

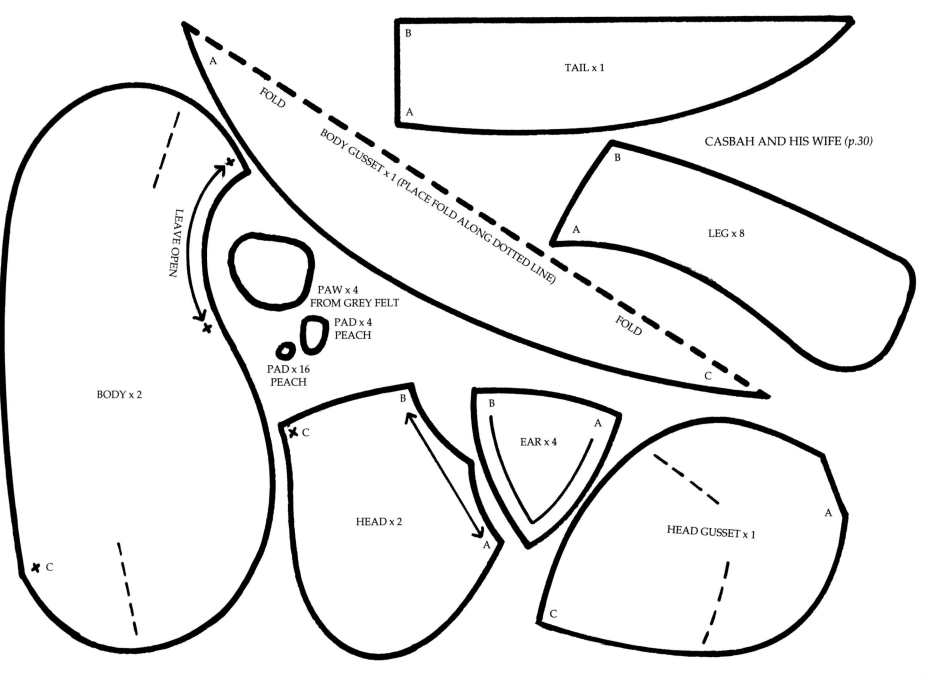

B

TAIL x 1

A

A

FOLD

CASBAH AND HIS WIFE *(p.30)*

B

BODY GUSSET x 1 (PLACE FOLD ALONG DOTTED LINE)

A

LEG x 8

LEAVE OPEN

FOLD

C

PAW x 4
FROM GREY FELT

PAD x 4
PEACH

PAD x 16
PEACH

BODY x 2

B

C

B

A

HEAD x 2

EAR x 4

A

HEAD GUSSET x 1

A

C

C

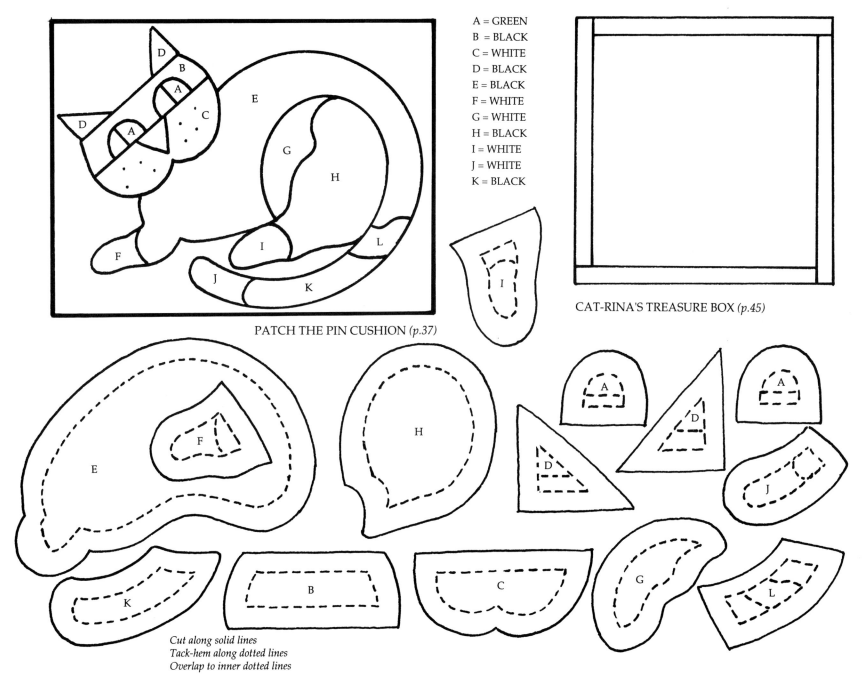

A = GREEN
B = BLACK
C = WHITE
D = BLACK
E = BLACK
F = WHITE
G = WHITE
H = BLACK
I = WHITE
J = WHITE
K = BLACK

PATCH THE PIN CUSHION (p.37)

CAT-RINA'S TREASURE BOX (p.45)

Cut along solid lines
Tack-hem along dotted lines
Overlap to inner dotted lines

SMOKEY THE NEEDLE CAT *(p.38)*

BIS-CAT TIN *(p.51)*

CAT TRA-IL *(p.55)*

CATS IN THE MOONLIGHT *(p.52)*

CUPPY-CAT *(p.53)*

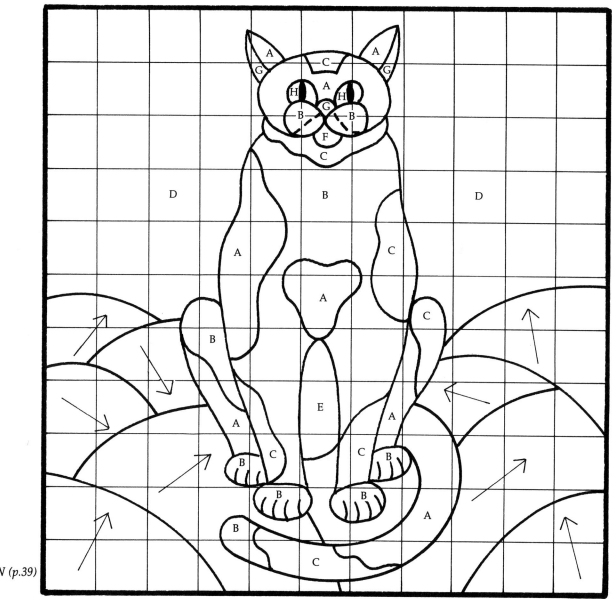

BLODWEN THE CAT-ER-PILLOW *(p.39)*
HAND-CAT-CHIEF *(p.55)*

BOARD CAT *(p.47)*

2 x.PAIR OF LEGS
5½in (14cm) SQUARE

1 x PAIR OF LEGS
4in (10½cm) SQUARE

2 x EAR
2¼in (6cm) SQUARE

CAT-CH *(p.31)*

2 x BODY (1 REVERSED)
FILL WITH 4oz
WHEAT
OR SIMILAR SEED

SEWING LINE

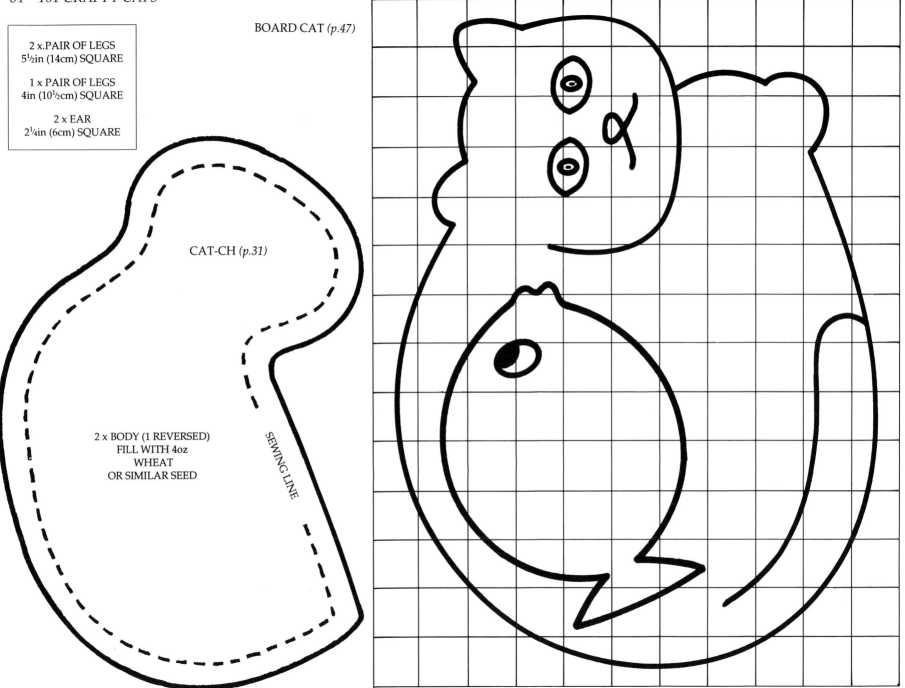

THE CAT'S WHISKERS *(p.37)*

GREEN PUNK CAT GOD *(p.59)*

CAT AT THE WINDOW *(p.60)*

CATMOBILE (p.48)
CAT WRAP (p.66)

*Measure against face
for making eye holes*

*For back piece,
cut along dotted line*

CAT MASK *(p.70)*

LINO CAT *(p.68)*

FAT CAT *(p.53)*
CAT CAKE *(p.74)*

A LETTER FROM YOUR CAT *(p.67)*

Stockist information

General craft supplies

You will find almost everything you need in good craft or art stores. However, there are two extremely good mail order companies who can supply you with the special paints, magnetic strip, cats' eyes, silk paints etc. described in this book. I suggest you obtain catalogues from both and what one doesn't have the other will.

Atlascraft Ltd., Ludlow Hill Road, West Bridgford, Nottingham NG2 6HD. Tel: 0602 360222/452202. In addition to general craft supplies, Atlascraft are the largest distributor of Deka specialist paints.

Fred Aldous Ltd., PO Box 135, 37 Lever Street, Manchester M60 1UX. Tel: 061 236 2477. Great for general crafts, lino cutting equipment, glass circles and magnetic tape.

Marabu silk paints, special effect pens and felt tips

Edding (UK) Ltd., Edding House, Merlin Centre, Acrewood Way, St Albans, Herts AL4 OJY. Tel: 0727 846688. Write for information on local stockists.

Silk ties and silk painting equipment

George Weil, The Warehouse, Reading Arch Road, Redhill, Surrey RH1 1HG. Tel: 0737 778868.

Embroidery, knitting and needlepoint requirements

Creativity, 45 New Oxford Street, London WC1A 1BH. Tel: 071 240 2945.

Greeting card blanks

Impress Cards, Slough Farm, Westhall, Halesworth, Suffolk IP19 8RN. Tel: 0986 781422.

Crayola Model Magic

Binney & Smith (Europe) Ltd., Ampthill Road, Bedford MK42 9RS. Tel: 0234 217786. Write for information on local stockists.

Toys-R-Us, Head Office, Geoffrey House, Van Wall Business Park, Van Wall Road, Maidenhead, Berks SL6 4UB. Tel: 0628 414141. Branches throughout the UK.

Fridge magnets

Bob Mitchell, 27 Archibald Street, Gloucester.

Booklist

In the course of her research, the author consulted the following books:

The Chatto Book of Cats, Francis Wheen (Chatto & Windus, 1993)

Lucinda Lambton's Magnificent Menagerie, Lucinda Lambton (Harper Collins, 1992)

The Cat Companion, Amy Shojai (Michael Friedman Publishing Group, 1992)

The Secret Life of Cats, Robert de Laroche and Jean-Michel Labat (Aurum Press, 1993)

The Life, History and Magic of the Cat, Fernand Méry (Paul Hamlyn, 1967)

The Complete Book of Cats, Judith A. Steeth (Bison Books, 1978)

The Complete Poems and Plays of T.S. Eliot (Faber & Faber, 1969)

The Brewer Dictionary of Phrase and Fable (Wordsworth Editions, 1993)

Brewers Myth and Legend, J.C. Cooper (Cassell, 1992)

Recommended reading:

How to Paint on Silk, Pam Dawson (Search Press, 1987)

The Dough Book, Tone Bergli Joner (Broadcast Books, 1991)

Papier Mâché, Susanne Haines (Charles Letts, 1990)

Character Cakes, Sandy Garfield (Sidgwick & Jackson, 1989)

Practical Decoupage, Denise Thomas and Mary Fox (Anaya, 1993)

101 Greeting Cards and How to Make Them, Melinda Coss (Aurum Press, 1993)

Paint Roses and Castles, Anne Young (David & Charles, 1992)

How to Draw Animals, Famous Artists School (Cortina Learning International, 1983)